Peter Simple's Century

By the same author:

Sheldrake

The Missing Will

A Dubious Codicil

The Stretchford Chronicles

Far Away is Close at Hand

Peter Simple's Century

Michael Wharton

The Claridge Press

Published in association with The Daily Telegraph

First published in Great Britain in 1999

by The Claridge Press
33 Canonbury Park South
London
N1 2JW

in association with The Telegraph Group Ltd

Printed by Antony Rowe Ltd
Chippenham

ISBN 1-870626-47-8

CIP data for this title is available from the British Library

Humour, Politics

Preface

The Peter Simple column first appeared in *The Daily Telegraph* in October 1955. Since then eleven collections of excerpts have been published at irregular intervals, as well as two collections marking 25 and 40 years respectively, published in 1980 and 1995.

Peter Simple's Century contains excerpts, originally published in *The Daily Telegraph* and *The Sunday Telegraph*, from 1987 to the present day. Satirical, polemical, fantastical or nonsensical, they are in roughly chronological order without any other arrangement.

Michael Wharton

Introduction

When Michael Wharton first took charge of the *Peter Simple* column in *The Daily Telegraph* more than 40 years ago, he can little have thought that it would see out the 20th Century. But so it is about to prove.

This is fitting, because there is no better witness to that century's follies than *Peter Simple*. Most articles that appear in newspapers are content to report or comment on what has just happened. Not *Peter Simple*. Again, and again, Wharton spotted something coming before it came. He invented the Race Relations Industry as a joke, and it soon became a phrase used without irony. He had the go-ahead Bishop of Bevindon supporting terrorism, witchcraft and homosexuality years before real, live bishops started to do the same. He spotted passive smoking, and has now introduced the forward-looking concept of passive drinking. Newspapers love to boast 'You read it here first'. With the *Peter Simple* column, that is the plain truth.

Indeed, if I were Michel Wharton I would be frightened at the way my comic fantasies and dark nightmares were so quickly fulfilled. Does he have a gift of prophecy, a paradoxical power to bring about what he most dreads? It is the sort of thought that might well vex his unquiet spirit.

But as the century draws to its close, and as the Millennium Dome offers a confection of nonsense that even Michel Wharton could not have imagined, the Peter Simple column can claim — to use a word it shuns — as much 'relevance' as ever. Collected in these pages is a choice of the finest and funniest thoughts about our age that have found their way into any newspaper in the world. Here are the legendary characters — Gen. 'Tiger' Nidgett of the Royal Army Tailoring Corps, Julian Birdbath and his unfinished life of Stephen Spender, Phantomsby, the last practising werewolf in the Midlands, and Mrs Dutt-Pauker in Marxmount, her millionaire Communist residence in Hampstead. Here is the British Boring Board of Control, the Chaplain to the Motorists' Liberation Front, the Aztec sit-in in the Stretchford Library and the Grey Book of Glynsabon.

An Editor is proud of many things in his newspaper — scoops, provocative comment, fine photographs, intrepid foreign reporting, but he does not often get the chance to boast that he publishes a work of art in weekly instalments. With *Peter Simple*, I can make that claim without exaggeration. His column and this, his Century, is a work of imagination. And, like all successful works of imagination, it is true.

Charles Moore,
Editor, *The Daily Telegraph*

Promising

A rally for about 1,500 deaf and dumb people organised by the British Deaf Association at Blackpool ended in a riot in which eight deaf and dumb people were arrested and four policemen hurt.

Most of the customs and rituals of the modern English riot seem to have been observed in a rather amateurish way: an ambulance was attacked (but not overturned); the rioters sprayed aerosol foam at each other and at passers-by; police reinforcements were called in from neighbouring towns and "came under a hail of bottles and cans".

A spokesman referred to this "appalling and regrettable incident" and added "as with soccer hooliganism, a small minority marred what was otherwise a trouble-free occasion. Our association will be looking at ways of preventing future trouble, like limiting the numbers or confining these events to our members only."

So far, so good. But as yet there are no reports of "copy cat" riots by the deaf and dumb in other places. Nor has any psychologist, not even Dr Kiosk, pronounced that the affray at Blackpool was "a cry for help, all the more urgent for being inarticulate, which our uncaring society will ignore at its peril".

There is a long way to go before a "small minority" like that of Blackpool becomes politicised and militant, claiming to represent the deaf and dumb community in general as victims of handicapism and institutionalised state violence, raising deaf and dumb consciousness all over the place and organising compulsory deafness and dumbness awareness work-shops for the hearing and articulate.

There is a long way to go. But if they do their duty the Blackpool Eight, though able to deliver protest slogans against police brutality only in sign Ianguage, can ensure that in due course the deaf and dumb take their proper place among the innumerable oppressed minorities of England

Cooking the Books

Cookery books, it is reported, are now being published at the rate of 11,000 a year. Inevitably, book-collectors who collect only cookery books are appearing. Many of them do not cook from the books they buy but merely read them. Do any of them cook and eat them?

One of the greatest rareties among cookery books, a real collector's item, is Julian Birdbath's "Book Cookery". This is a collection of recipes made by the unfortunate author who discovered the "missing Brontë sister" Doreen, one of the greatest feats of literary detection in history, and followed it up by discovering a whole series of other "missing Brontë sisters" including Dawn, Linda, Tracy, and Denise, and even a "missing Brontë brother", Dwight.

In his early days in Deadwater Leadmine (disused) near Bakewell, where Birdbath lives with his pet toad, Amiel, he was reduced to cooking and eating the review copies he had retained from his life above ground, together with remaindered copies of his own "Quest for Doreen Brontë", "Doreen Brontë: the Formative Years" and other books which "fell dead from the press".

His neighbour Mr Shuttleworth, a poultry-farmer and part-time literary agent, occasionally shovels loads of unreadable books, relics of rectory libraries and such, down the shaft and Birdbath now subsists mainly on these. That is how he has become an expert on book cookery and why Mr Shuttleworth, in exchange for a small advance, which he retained, was able to induce the Toadstone Press to commission Birdbath to write a book on the subject some years ago.

"Book Cookery" also failed, receiving few reviews and those contemptuous ("Pitiful drivel" *Catering Times*). So Birdbath was reduced to cooking and eating remaindered copies of his own book.

He finished his last copy only the other day, fried with strange toadstools of the mine and garnished with glue from the binding of Volume Eight of the Rev Mungo MacCanister's *Collected Sermons* (1892).

By a supreme irony, at the very moment when Birdbath was finishing his grim repast, a copy of his book (immaculate, with original dustjacket) was knocked down at Sotheby's to an American collector of modern first editions for a record sum of £150,000.

Ominous

The Ayatollah Khomeini, it must be admitted, is not a popular figure in this country. His stern expression, beetling brows and generally uncompromising demeanour repel rather than attract. Photographs, which are all most of us have to go on, may, of course be misleading. In his hours of leisure, probably few, he may be delightful company, setting low dinner-tables in a roar with jokes about President Reagan. He may be adored as well as respected by his own family and a great success with small children.

Even in England he has his admirers. Last year several typical Stretchford housewives, expelled even from the Anti-Our Auntie Garoufalidis (Revisionist) Fan Club for excessive ferocity and "motiveless incendiarism" formed an Our Ayatollah Khomeini Fan Club. They wore *chadors* at all times, adopting a threatening mien in super-markets and causing Supt J. S. Harrogate, 49, the police fan club supremo, to quote "Omar Khayyam" in a low, worried tone to his cat Fluff, 8.

Mrs Linda Vehicle 57, head of the OAKFC, wrote a letter to the Ayatollah c/o The General Post Office, Qom, asking him for permission to declare a *jihad* (or holy war) against all the other fan clubs. But to her disgust the letter was returned, marked in Persian, French and English "Not Known at this Address".

After that the club disintegrated and now only Mrs Vehicle herself is left, still wearing her *chador* and dreaming of what might have been.

However, Mr J. H. Purgatroyd, 62, a native of the West Riding who retired to Nerdley for undisclosed reasons only last year, has now formed an Ayatollah Khomeini Fan Club which meets every Thursday evening in his house in Kandahar Road for soda water and cheese sandwiches. Some members believe their hero is a reincarnation of Alderman Foodbotham.

"You can say what you like about the Ayatollah," Mr Purgatroyd says, "but I can tell you one thing: he's a man who knows his own mind, choose how. It certainly makes you pensive."

Mr Purgatroyd denies that he is paid by unknown sources in the West Riding, possibly the Mafia, to talk in this way. His headquarters, by an ominous coincidence, are only a short way from the Friends of Genghis Khan just up the road on the corner of Canalshaw Drive. Police are monitoring the situation.

Gone to Earth

"You're useless! You're pathetic! You're dead unhip! You aren't even a gender-bender! When did you last crash out on coke — or anything else? Do you know what you remind me of? Somebody out of the Middle Ages like St Augustus! Though I dare say old Gus — he was African, wasn't he? — had more zip and fun and glitz about him than you have, you zonked out old wimp!"

Thus upbraided by Cliff Rampton, his chief manager, in the £4 million Ionic white and gold audience hall of his £150 million castle in Sussex, Ron Frabb, the 47-year-old teenage idol, collapsed on the steps of his £1 million ivory and onyx throne, sobbing bitterly.

It was not the first time his manager had compared Ron unfavourably with "Madonna" and even less glittering stars now enchanting the world with the lewd howlings of financial genius. But it may have been the last.

Next morning, when Ron's £2 million blonde chief personal nurse parted the curtains of white samite round his 24-feet-wide, £6 million gold and lapis lazuli bed to offer him a selection of his favourite pills, she found that he had gone!

Alarm bells sounded in all parts of the castle — at any rate in some. Like everything else in Frabb's domains the alarm system is not what it was. Signs of decay — moth and rust and worse — are everywhere. Even the marble pillars in the £5 million entrance hall, through which so many devout pilgrims from all over the world once passed, are cracked in places. Part of the £1 million ceiling has fallen down.

On the marble terrace the flowers wither in their storied urns. Out in the enormous park rank grasses and weeds infest the sacred turf where so many great ones have yelled and gibbered. Of the eight lodges, only one is now inhabited, and — supreme irony — by a classical pianist on the run!

Where is the grieving teenage idol, still master of a great though diminished empire of cacophony? "I couldn't care less. I'm through!" said Rampton, as he filled suitcase after suitcase with costly relics, muttering to himself "£7 million ... £14 million ... £21 million ..." in unconscious arithmetical progression.

But where is Ron? some say he has been glimpsed among the screaming hordes around "Madonna", clumsily disguised with inch-thick make-up as a 10-year-old groupie. Some say he was seen among the celebrants greeting the arrival of the New Age of Aquarius on Glastonbury Tor, wearing silken robes and a cardboard crown and adding his uncertain personal humming to the Great Hum of Peace.

Shall we ever know his fate? Can it be that he has been incorporated, by means we cannot understand, into some myriad-selling "single" and so, for all Rampton's taunts, is truly in the groove for ever?

Round the Clubs

The Old Thanateum Club, or "Thanners" as everyone calls it (*writes "Clubman"*), is still doing sterling work by taking in London clubs which have lost their own premises. With the recent addition of the Geographers ("Joggers"), the Sandwich ("Sanners") and Peppers ("Peppers"), it now houses no fewer than 32 clubs which have as it were fallen by the wayside.

The result is that the fine old building in Pall Mall is getting decidedly overcrowded. There is an ominous bulge in the library wall and only the other day a whole shelf-full of heavy leather-bound books fell into the street, narrowly missing passers-by and leaving a gaping hole in the wall.

"Trouble is," Major "Jock" Gapwright-Jones ("Gappers"), the club secretary, tells me, "that the chap from Westminster Council who keeps coming round now has an additional grouse. As you know, Jim, the club wyvern, had a baby, Fred, last summer — don't ask me how, there are some things it's better not to pry into when you're dealing with fabulous monsters — so what with the two of them setting fire to things the smoke gets thicker all the time.

He broke off for a fit of coughing in which I joined. "This council chap says that as well as the wyverns being a fire hazard the whole place is an environmental hazard and a bad case of inner city overcrowding. He even talked, last time he called, of an eviction order, as though we were a lot of slum-dwellers behind with the rent.

"I had a good laugh when young Fred — he's a mischievous little beggar, very bright for his age, and we all love him dearly — scampered up and set this blighter's briefcase on fire. Couldn't see his feet for dust, in fact you couldn't see him at all," laughed "Gappers", as we both doubled up coughing and one of the bow-windows collapsed into the street, taking several elderly members with it.

Forebodings

On March 16, the *Catholic Herald* celebrates its centenary. To go back a bit, its comments of July 18, 1941 on the pact just concluded between the British and Soviet Governments have a painful interest:

"The more we look at this treaty the less we like it ... We have apparently undertaken to share .Mr Churchill's 'new freedom and glory for all mankind' — he had just used this high-flown phrase in one of his speeches — "in association with a Government whose avowed and never-renounced policy is ... aggression by underhand and conspiratorial methods against what remains of Christianity and civilisation."

It was quite courageous to print things like that in the England of that time, and it seems that the Prime Minister was in fact angry enough to consider suppressing the newspaper and imprisoning the editor, Michael de la Bedoyere.

We know now what the outcome of that pact was and how much freedom and glory it brought to mankind. Credit is due to those who did not like it then and dared to say so.

A Really Nice Coven

The British Witchcraft Council of Elders has decided not to have a new king after the death of Mr Alex Sanders, who reigned for 25 years. His widow, Maxine, says that in former times the king was sacrificed after seven years. That has stopped, she explains, "but nobody in their right mind wanted the job".

Mrs Elvira Mutcliffe, who runs a much-respected coven near Sowerby Bridge in the West Riding, said yesterday that Mrs Sanders' remarks were "in very poor taste" and "not in the best interests of witchcraft today".

Mrs Mutcliffe's own coven, which meets on Tuesdays at her semi-detached home "in a very nice part of the locality" for a light tea of potted meat sandwiches and assorted pastries within the magic pentacle, has no connection with the Council of Elders, and Mrs Mutcliffe has never recognised the king.

She thinks ending the practice of sacrificing the king after seven years was "a definite lowering of standards" and made it difficult for properly qualified witches to take the council seriously. "The sacrifice could be a really lovely thing if it was done in a tasteful, refined way."

At her last coven meeting Cllr Albert Gogden, the Head Warlock and Keeper of the Trilby Hat of Invisibility, annoyed her by hinting that he was thinking of applying for the job of Witch King in succession to Mr Sanders. "Well, Albert, if you do, I'm afraid you will no longer be welcome in my coven. I have certain standards to keep up," she said, slapping his wrist as he reached rudely over the table for a particular pastry he had had his eye on for some time. Shamefaced, he assumed the Hat and immediately vanished.

"And please take your hat off when ladies are present", Mrs Mutcliffe said.

"Really! Manners."

Election Prospects

For all the changes in the Soviet Union, the General Election Mr Gorbachev, leader of the Liberal party, hinted at nearly two years ago seems as far off as ever. We hear a great deal (writes a Political Expert) about the struggle between Mr Gorbachev's Liberal party and the Conservative party led by Mr Yegor Ligachev. Less known outside the Soviet Union are the manoeuvrings of the numerous "centre parties" as they try to secure what the Russians call the "middle ground" (characterised by the untranslatable Russian word "midnost").

It is thought there are between 80 and 100 of these small parties, all descended, in the last analysis (a rough equivalent of the untranslatable Russian "analysnost"), from the old Liberal party which played such an important part in the Duma before the First World War.

This power struggle for the "middle ground" is one of shifting alliances and bewildering changes of nomenclature where key figures seem to emerge momentarily from the mêlée only to be lost again. There are the Social Democrats, the Liberal Democrats, the Liberal and Social Democrats, the Democratic Liberals, the Social Liberals and dozens more, all with ambitious leaders constantly changing from one party to another in a frenzy of backbiting which amazes ordinary Soviet citizens used to the calm political atmosphere of the days before perestroika.

Will Ivan Nembutalov, leader of the Social and Liberal Democrats and a direct descendant of the 19th century anarcho-syndicalist philosopher Pyotr Nembutalov, succeed in ousting Andrei Diazepamov, formerly of the Liberal and Social Democrats, now leader of the Democratic Liberals, and build a combined Liberal, Social, Democratic, Liberal and Social party?

Has Fyodor Limbritolov, leader and sole member of the Democratic Social Liberals, a political future at all? These are some of the questions the Soviet Man in the Street is asking himself as he slumps heavily to the ground in an ecstasy of boredom (the untranslatable "narkonost")?

The leaders of the two big parties affect to regard these centre parties as irrelevant, able to draw only on the "protest vote" — "protestnost" as it is untranslatably called. Yet they both fear the ultimate nightmare: that a combination of small parties might hold the balance of power in a "hung Duma", leading to a second General Election whose outcome no man could foresee.

Cast a Cold Eye

There used to be an old joke in the literary bars of Dublin that when the entire Irish Navy was sent to bring back Yeats's bones from France in 1948 for reburial in his native Sligo, the gunboat, through an error, brought back the bones of a grocer instead.

Now it turns out that the bones are not even those of a grocer, but the mingled bones of Yeats and several French paupers, buried like him — and this is a strange thing in itself — in an "economy grave".

The proud poet, who scorned the middle sort, would have preferred the paupers to the grocer. But does it matter whose bones lie in the churchyard of Drumcliffe, with that famous epitaph on the gravestone, where now — another of time's cruel ironies — few who pay tribute and pass by are likely to be horsemen?

As with the Holy Shroud, it is belief that counts. There is a Tibetan story of a young monk who was given the task of carrying a particularly holy tooth, the relic of a saint, to a distant monastery but lost it by the wayside. Terrified, he substituted a dog's tooth and presented that instead.

After a while, installed in a splendid reliquary and greatly venerated the dog's tooth began to glow with supernatural light and perform miracles, proof, as the saying was, that even a dog's tooth will shine brightly in the eye of faith.

On the Frontier

A report from Southwark Council's Race Equality Committee, "Racial Language and Terminology", gives some interesting definitions. Thus, "race equality" is defined as "To make races equal. With some more equal than others, due to the phenomenological state of affairs, i.e., black minorities in a homogenous white society, race equality can only attempt to proportionate."

A counsel of despair. Yet under the heading "anti-racism" we have: "utilising the term 'race' in no matter how positive a manner (eg in terms like 'multi-racial education') validates the basic ideas upon which racism builds. Policy-makers must therefore abandon any such usage; instead, policy should be developed which attacks the idea that there are such things as races. Policy must be *anti-racist*, not multi-racial".

A hard saying. For if the term "race" is not to be used, can such terms as "race equality" be used either? And should there be any such thing as a "race equality committee"?

Here we are treading on the frontiers of knowledge. Here is the domain of "race relations theory", or "higher race relations" as they call it among the cloud-capped towers of Ethnic House, the race relations industry's majestic London Headquarters. Here the finest minds in the industry are working towards the long sought "unified field theory" which will show that everything in the universe, from the smallest particle to the largest supernova, is both "racist" and "anti-racist" at one and the same time — if time it can be called.

Aztec Studies

The Aztec community in Nerdley is demanding that children in primary schools should be taught about "Aztec religion and culture". Cllr. J.S. Duttcliffe, chairman of the Education Committee, has promised support. Since the Aztecs first appeared in Nerdley in 1965, occupying a public library and claiming it as one of the sites colonised by Aztecs in the Dark Ages after crossing the Atlantic in stone boats, the community has grown in numbers. Present estimates of "ethnic Aztecs" vary between three and 25,000.

Royston Vibes, their leader, a 40-year-old, Middlesbrough born 28th-year sociology student at Nerdley University, welcomes Cllr Duttcliffe's support. Although it is believed there are very few, indeed no, Aztec pupils in primary schools in the borough, he thinks some knowledge of Aztec history, language and customs will help to counter prejudice and discrimination.

"We resent the patronising, even downright hostile, attitude of some people towards Aztecs," he says. "Only the other day one of our people, Fred Tove, a Scunthorpe-born sociology student at the university, was going about his ordinary business with a rope threaded through his tongue when a group of hooligans — probably merchant bankers — began jeering and throwing lager cans at him.

"We do not ask for favoured treatment, only for compassion and understanding. We also demand Aztec Sections in the Labour party, representation in the General Synod of the Church of England, Britain's withdrawal from Nato, release of the Nerdley 27,819 (est.) and British troops out of Ireland."

Several parents have threatened to remove their children from school if "Aztec studies" go ahead. "I am not racist but a firm believer in live and let live," said Mrs Linda Yells, 29, who has two children at Carbon Road Primary School, "but as far as my kids are concerned I do not approve of human sacrifice". Her husband, Mr S.J. Yells, 32, an unemployed turntable underlooker, was less definite but said he "probably agreed in principle."

"With this sort of attitude," Cllr Duttcliffe said, "we obviously have a very long way to go before we can say we are living in a truly multi-cultural Britain."

Wiser Counsels

Police in Communist China have discovered a flourishing trade in mentally retarded women, who are much in demand as peasants' wives because they are thought to be obedient and unlikely to run away.

A Marriage Guidance Counsellor writes: Although it is illegal to buy wives in England, whether mentally retarded or not, mentally retarded wives can of course be found in the ordinary way and have some of the same advantages as those in China.

However, it would be unwise to think that mentally retarded wives are a guarantee of marital happiness. Though obedient enough, they may be unable to understand a husband's verbal orders clearly. And as they tend to be wholly or partially illiterate, it is futile for the husband to write out daily orders and pin them up on a noticeboard.

I have known cases where marriages "drifted on the rocks" because a mentally retarded wife was unable to clean her husband's shoes properly, wasted coke by spilling it on the stairs while bringing it up from the cellar or could not even understand that in order to scale a large domestic boiler it is necessary to get inside it!

Another disadvantage of mentally retarded wives in this country is that they are more suggestible and easily influenced than the average woman. They may, for instance, fall a prey to militant feminists (themselves often mentally retarded) and so turn into militant feminists themselves, all the more aggressive because of their poor reasoning ability.

One of the most distressing examples in my casebook was a couple — a husband of average intelligence and a mentally retarded wife — who for a time were blissfully happy. Then the wife, who could read newspapers, found out about the campaign for women priests in the Church of England. Encouraged by local feminists, she told everyone she met that she was going to be a bishop.

Marital discord naturally developed. The end came when she managed to get a complete Episcopal outfit — cope, mitre, crozier and so on — through a feminist mail order catalogue and was arrested while dressed as a bishop and trying to hold a service in a local supermarket. I'm afraid I see little hope of a reconciliation.

All Yours

A team of futurologists — futurology is a "science" of unmistakably American provenance — has produced a forecast of what this country will be like 21 years from now. It predicts a "fundamental international change in social values, beliefs and norms", a "paradigm shift from the materialistic to a general consciousness that people matter more".

Home computers will be the nerve-centres of households; genetic screening of pregnant women will be common; there will be holidays on the moon; one credit card will pay for goods and services throughout Western Europe; education will be by "high-speed, high-information games"; home image-generators will produce, for example, the illusion of walking along the Great Wall of China; there will be a second Channel Tunnel and automated road and rail traffic systems; and so on and so forth.

In all this glittering fantasy of technological progress there is not one word about what really matters to human beings. There is nothing which has to do with the true concerns of life and death. There is only the promise of more and yet more of the ever-proliferating toys and gadgets and illusions we already have in such abundance. Where is the "paradigm shift" here? Where is the change in values, beliefs and norms?

Who in his heart wants such a tawdry future? Who in his heart does not rejoice that it will never come about, or, if it does, will soon collapse under its own intolerable weight of lies, in unimaginable ruin?

Round the Salerooms

There was brisk bidding at Gotheby's yesterday when several important animal pictures came up for auction, reflecting the current vogue both for animal iconography and for Victorian sentiment.

A large painting in oils by William Garbuthnot (1810-1903); The Old Game-keeper's Last Mourners, showing a coffin surrounded by a group of animals including half a dozen dogs of various breeds, three cats, several rabbits, stoats, squirrels, jackdaws and crows and — an unusual touch of irony — a small crocodile, went for £25,500 to the well-known Armenian collector Sarkis Vegetarian.

Good Friends, a water colour by Emily Pencil (1881-1920), a minor member of the Porthfrantick School, showing a Newfoundland dog wearing a frock coat and sharing a large plate of porridge with a Shetland pony, with a background of Cornish cliffs, was knocked down for £16,000 to an anonymous bidder.

Charge! (also entitled Nova Scotia, Here We Come!), a spirited oil by the Scottish artist Hamish McCough, one of the so-called "Gorbals Boys", showing an evicted Highland family pursued by a pack of Clackmannanshire terriers while in the background a grinning land agent dynamites their homestead, went for £28,000 to another Armenian collector, Nubar Antediluvian.

A huge canvas, 16 feet by 20, by the West Riding historical painter Marsden Grindrod, known as "the Tintoretto of the North Midlands", formerly the property of Alderman Jabez Foodbotham, showing Hannibal, one of the Alderman's black carriage horses, which he appointed Town Clerk of Bradford in 1919, presiding at a finance committee meeting, failed to reach its reserve.

At once the saleroom darkened as a black storm cloud formed near the ceiling, a chasm opened in the floor and a thunderous voice which seemed to come from everywhere and nowhere announced that anybody who jumped into it would get the biggest surprise of his life.

Sporting times

State politicians in Florida are trying to make the sport of dwarf-throwing, which has become popular in the American South, illegal. A spokesman for the World Dwarf-throwing Authority comments:

"Ever since this essentially clean, healthy and invigorating sport originated in the bars of the Australian Outback it has had to face much unfair criticism. It has been described as "medieval," as though this was a valid objection. We have only to think of such medieval sports as grinning through a horse-collar, hanging by the heels from the rafters or competitive boiled egg eating to appreciate their character-forming qualities.

"In the early days abuses undoubtedly occurred. Betting was rife until brought under control by the World Dwarf-throwing Authority's Betting Regulation Board in 1978. As for charges of cruelty and bad taste, no dwarf may now be thrown (Rule 45) without his written consent."

Alas!

The Centenary of the birth of Sir Stafford Cripps has passed with remarkably little excitement. Here and there a parade, ranks sadly thinned, of veteran enforcement officers holding plastic replicas of pork pies impounded as in excess of rationing entitlement; here and there a ceremonial power-cut or furtive switching on of one bar of an electric fire; or, in some musty saloon bar, an old man's ritual repetition of the terrible joke (attributed to Churchill) on Cripps's name: that is about all.

Can the Master of Austerity be forgotten so soon, or worse, not even known at all to a thoughtless and ignorant generation? For us, whose later youth was spent in the days of his greatness, the post-war Chancellor of Attlee's Labour Government has become (who would have thought it?) a figure imbued with hopeless longing. Or has he? Speak for yourself.

Well, for me at any rate, a newspaper photograph showing Bishop Mervyn Stockwood, along with Mr Michael Foot and Lord Longford, standing outside the house in Chelsea where Cripps was born, after the Bishop had unveiled a memorial plaque, was unbearably poignant.

The three old stalwarts of an extinct kind of socialism, the curtained window, the brick wall, the very drainpipe — all seemed to have receded into a time immeasurably remote; to be one not with Nineveh and Tyre (places notoriously lacking in rationing schemes and most unacceptable to Cripps) but with the dust and shards of pre-history.

Does that time call us back from our days of heedless plenty? Would we relish the cardboard taste of gravy in a British Restaurant? Treasure sweet tokens and furniture dockets? Exult over our allowance of £25 in foreign currency? Gladly exchange, knowing what we know, our noisy, vulgar, dangerous, cosmopolitan time for a time when — although the pitifully emaciated figure of a socialist John Bull on Ministry of Labour posters exhorted us to "work or want" — England was still England?

A Treat in Store

The newly published *Letters of Leonard Woolf* includes not one single item from the correspondence between the great colonial civil servant, publisher and husband of Virginia Woolf, and S. J. Barstow (1886-1929), the only hydro-electrical engineering member of the Bloomsbury group.

Has blind anti-electrical prejudice been at work again, seeking to extinguish all memory of "Basil" Barstow, as everybody called him, at Garsington, though his real name was Stanley? A contemporary of D. H. Lawrence at Nottingham University, he later studied at the Slade. But he had already had mystical intimations, of his life's work: to create a synthesis between art and hydro-electrical engineering.

He had already published his seminal "Hydro-Electrical Engineering: a New Art Form" when Lawrence introduced him to Ottoline Morrell in 1925. Soon he was a frequent guest at her house parties and became a general favourite with his "amusing" tricks, such as generating hydroelectrical power in a teapot and passing current through a Japanese screen to light up a very weak electric bulb a few feet away, invariably causing Lytton Strachey to swoon with emotion.

It was not long before Leonard Woolf realised the important part Barstow could play in his publishing schemes. Soon the brilliant young engineer was in great demand, often changing several electric light bulbs a week as well as mending fuses and fitting an ingenious hydro-electric alarm bell which rang every time a junior employee of the Hogarth Press tried to appropriate even a single sheet of paper or a paper-clip for his own use.

Much of the correspondence between Woolf and Barstow is concerned with such matters. But it rises to the heights of epistolary art in eloquent exchanges in which Woolf vainly urges Barstow to join the Fabian Society while Barstow urges Woolf, even more vainly, to settle outstanding bills for fuse wire, labour and overtime. It deserves a volume to itself, and, it is to be hoped, will soon get one.

Unhelpful

Mr Brendan O'Friel, the governor of Strangeways Prison, described the violence there as "an explosion of evil". "Well, of course, that's not really very helpful," commented a penologist on a television programme later on, with a pitying smile.

I cannot remember what he thought *would* be helpful. No doubt it was one of the innumerable "solutions to the problem" we have heard over the last few weeks. They range from the abolition of prisons altogether to more compulsory drama classes or more facilities for prisoners to learn to work computers instead of sewing mailbags, on the ground (doubtful to say the least) that this will fit them better for life in the outer world on their release.

Any television verbaliser is apt to dismiss a belief in evil as unhelpful and absurd, if not élitist, or even fascist. But it may be that not to believe in evil, whether in prison or in the outer world, is just about the most absurd and unhelpful thing there is.

The Nerdley Tapes

The "bugging device" which some years ago I had installed in the panel-beating section of the Boggs Motorworks at Nerdley, which produces such famous cars as the Boggs Yobbo and Super-Oaf, is still working. Here is a short extract from recent tapes, evidently recorded during a tea break. I have, of course, altered the names of the speakers.

Jim: Good morning, Fred. I trust you are well? (Noise of chuckling, turning into laughter). Good heavens, my dear fellow! You seem to be in a state of unwonted hilarity. What, may I ask, is that volume you are perusing?

Fred (splutters): It is called *The Satanic Verses*, by Salman Rushdie.

Jim: But, Fred, it is no laughing matter. I have not read the book in question, but I am told that parts of it at least are highly improper. I do aver that if Mr Harrison, our esteemed shop steward, were to find you reading it he would confiscate the volume immediately.

Fred: I'd like to see him try. It is the most amusing book I have read since *Three Men in a Boat*, my boyhood favourite.

Jim: For shame, Fred. Can you not find something to read of a more improving nature than these? Samuel Smiles is still my favourite. Besides, I have heard that poor Mr Rushdie is in a desperate plight, condemned to death by Muslim fundamentalists and forced into hiding none knows where. Why, for all I know, he may be not a hundred miles from this very place.

Fred: I would dearly love to meet him.

Jim: Quick, Fred, put the book away. Here, if I am not greatly mistaken, comes our popular Asian workmate Rashid Patel. He must not see it on any account. Nay, Fred, it is no laughing matter. Make haste. Good morning, Rashid.

Rashid: Good morning, lads, one and all. Do not rattle your brains, Fred, I have myself perused volume in question.

Fred, Jim: You, Rashid!

Rashid: Yes, I am multi-racial and ecumenical. I am spirit of modern Britain. I am opposed to all forms of intolerance. My name, as you will realise, is not both Hindu and Muslim for nothing. I earnestly uphold Mr Rushdie's right to free speech. I also earnestly uphold offended Muslim people's right to condemn him to death. So, Fred, I must regretfully relieve you of the volume so that I may set fire to it. Jim, may I borrow your matches?

Fred: Oh no you don't! I don't care what you say! Keep off! It's mine! (Bursts into tears; sound of heavy boots approaching.)

Jim: Hush, you two! If I am not deceived, it is Mr Harrison himself.

Mr Harrison: What is the meaning of this unseemly uproar? In a statutory tea-break, too. Come, lads, pull yourselves together. Hand me that book.

All: Yes, Mr Harrison.

Mr Harrison: Ah, *The Satanic Verses*. I have long wished to peruse it, for I am partial to the post-modernist, magical realist school of literature (begins reading to himself, instantly giving way to chuckles and soon to roars of laughter).

Dangerous Ground

M Jean-Marie Le Pen, leader of the French National Front party, has been ordered to pay a symbolic fine for having told an interviewer three years ago that the question of the gas chambers was "a mere detail of the Second World War". If you consider the cold statistics of overall killings in that war, which included Hiroshima, the bombing of Germany, the atrocities of Stalin and enormous massacres on all sides, a detail it certainly was.

But in a historical sense, what a detail! The Nazis' attempt to exterminate the Jews, whether or not it was an evil absolutely unique in human history, has had one effect Hitler himself could not have anticipated: for 50 years it has made it unacceptable not merely to criticise the Jews adversely but even to discuss their place in the world in the impartial way any other interesting and important matters — and what is more interesting or important than the history of the Jews? — can be discussed. Even to suggest such a thing may bring (as now) accusations of "anti-Semitism".

Is this special position of privilege a good thing at a time when the power of the Jews in the world has never been greater; when the State of Israel may hold the fate of the world in its hands? Is it a good thing for the Jews themselves that no-one may suggest, even for the sake of argument, that their power may not always, everywhere and in every way, be exercised for good?

Sensible Drinking

"Hooray!" shouted 14-year-old Jim Smith, as his parents John and Mary Smith, his elder brother Tom, aged 17, and 19-year-old sister Betty filed into the Sensible Drinking Room. "Thanks to the Health Education Authority and Alcohol Concern;" said Jim, "it's Sensible Drinking Day again! 1 wonder what I'll start with this time? A glass of wine? A half-pint of ordinary strength beer or lager? A measure of spirits? A small sherry? Or shall I mix them all together?"

"Don't be silly, Jim," said Betty.

"That's four units out of your weekly quota of 21 units straight off. You'd only have 17 left. Besides, if you mix them all up you'll probably be sick."

"No I shan't," said Jim defiantly. "Only the other day I drank a whisky and sherry together as well as a low-alcohol rum, and I wasn't sick at all. So there!"

"Was that two units or did the low-alcohol rum make it three?" asked Tom, who had a methodical turn of mind. "Two!" "Three!" "Two and a half!" "You don't count halves!" "Yes, you do, stupid!" "It says here in the Alcohol Concern handbook...." "No, it doesn't!" "Drop dead!"

"Now children, children — I mean kids," said John. "Stop quarrelling or we'll never get our Sensible Drinking started at all." "We'll never learn to enjoy ourselves drinking sensibly and not putting ourselves and other people at risk," said Mary. "What's the good of the Government giving all that extra money to the Health Education Authority and Alcohol Concern if we don't do what they tell us?" said John.

"Well, here goes," said Mary. "I'm going to start off with a small sherry." She poured one out of the decanter into a glass and began sipping very slowly, hardly more than one drop at a time. "One unit," said Tom, watching closely. John poured himself a half-pint of beer. "Are you sure that's ordinary Strength?" asked Betty. John was so upset by her suspicious attitude that he drank his beer, poured himself another and drank that off in one go.

"Two units there," said Tom. "I say, Dad, you're going it a bit today, aren't you?" "Well, I'm still sensible," said John. "And that's more than can be said for some." "What do you mean by that?" snapped Mary, who had started on her second sherry. She drank it much more quickly than the first.

Meanwhile Betty had drunk one small gin, a non-alcoholic Pernod and a glass of wine, marking two units on her handy pocket alcohol-unit calculator. Jim had now drunk a half-pint of ordinary strength beer, a glass of wine, a non-alcoholic cherry brandy and a non-alcoholic vodka.

"You've all had two units each already," said Tom smugly. He had been calculating their units but not drinking anything himself. "I say, that's not fair," Jim shouted. "How can you drink sensibly if you don't drink anything?" "Shut up, fish-face!" "Shut up yourself!"

"Look here, all of you," said Mary. "We're supposed to be enjoying ourselves learning to drink sensibly as a family, not quarrelling all the time. I've had enough of this!" "Well, I haven't," said John, drinking five glasses of sherry, three glasses of beer (ordinary strength) and 11 measures of Irish whiskey, the rest of his 21 units for that week, and immediately slumping heavily to the ground. The rest of them soon followed his example.

Enchantment

A Manifesto from Dr Kalim Siddiqui, described as the controversial director of the Muslim Institute, calls on British Muslims to set up their own separate government as part of a "non-territorial state" in the United Kingdom. This has not gone down well either with non-Muslim commentators or with more moderate Muslims.

Yet the idea will appeal to all lovers of the picturesque and of the quaint anomalies of history. Why should this Muslim State be non-territorial? It should have its own territory somewhere in this country, an enclave like Gibraltar or lamented Goa, so cruelly snatched by the rapacious Indians after centuries of harmless separate existence. The world must not grow too neat and tidy.

With its exotic customs, its veiled women, its bearded imams and Koranic scholars, its splendid mosques, its arcades and gardens of roses, bulbuls and fountains rivalling those of Moorish Spain, this new Islamic state would be a place of wonder and enchantment.

For us non-Muslims, the excluded, it might become a place of hopeless longing. Dr Siddiqui rightly condemns the "corrupt bog-land of Western culture", and his would be a land free of the plagues of television, howling pop festivals and every kind of debased art and entertainment.

Perhaps, after all, this paradise had better be "non-territorial"; otherwise there would be such a rush to escape into it that Dr Siddiqui's original ideal would soon be ruined.

War Fever

America's appeal to its allies in Nato to support its forces in Saudi Arabia has brought an immediate response from one of them at any rate: Great Britain. But there is some doubt about what kind of forces we should send. In the Stretchford Conurbation, where war fever is mounting hourly, there is an insistent demand that elements of the Royal Stretchfordshire Yeomanry, if not the whole lot, should be included.

This venerable regiment has been described as "a veritable inferno of age-old tradition". Its mess customs alone occupy more than 80 pages, including tables of precedence and vector analysis of port-circulation and snuff-taking procedures, in the new edition of the present adjutant Capt T. R. B. St X St Q Haggard-Jelkes's regimental history.

Many people think that once the Yeomanry settled down in Saudi

Arabia with its regimental silver and other essential equipment and started regular guest nights, it could do a lot to offset the somewhat unfortunate impression the brash Americans, with their rage for everything new, must be making on the courteous sheikhs and other conservatively inclined Sons of the Desert.

Even the regiment's veteran mess-waiters might find, unlikely as it may seem, that they had much in common with the cupbearers, eunuchs and other servants of the Saudi nobility.

Another suggestion is that additional British forces should include a contingent of the Royal Army Tailoring Corps, brainchild of the military genius Gen Sir Frederick ("Tiger") Nidgett, whose exploits in the Second World War are still talked of with fear and derision in the bazaars of Port Said. With its experience of fast-moving urban desert warfare, the Corps would make an invaluable contribution.

Headed by Sgt Maj Trousercutter Stan ("Jock") Lazarowicz, scion of a distinguished Edinburgh family and former chairman of the Ratcorps Veterans' Association, they are offering their services to the Defence Ministry in droves.

"I'm no troublemaker, ye ken", says Jock impulsively, "but if the lads don't get a guid look in on this desert show I'll no' answer for the consequences. They're mad keen and rarin' to go, that's for sure," he added with an unconscious echo of the conversational style of the RATC's great founder.

Its crack Special Embroidery Units, which were disbanded in one of the Government's retrenchment schemes some years ago, should be reconstituted, he thinks. They could give magnificent service by helping to smarten up the head-dresses of the Saudi officer corps and adding those little decorative touches to the hems of their splendid white robes which make all the difference to morale in modern warfare in the desert.

At his laurel-infested home at Godalming the "Tiger" would only say: "It's early days yet." But as his piercing blue eyes seemed to peer into the infinite sands of Arabia, he could be heard humming beneath his breath the stirring anthem of the "Lads with the Needles and Thread", *Thimbles Awa'*!

Before long that sound may be striking terror into the pitch-black heart of Saddam, who will soon wish, as the Germans did of old, that the Royal Army Tailoring Corps had never been invented.

A Guilty Library

A public library in High Wycombe, known as the "fortress" or "pillbox" from its wire-mesh window defences, has been closed down because of incessant attacks by youths with stones, bricks and other missiles and threats of assaults on the staff. "As far as we know," says the County Librarian, "this is the only country library in England to be closed in such circumstances."

Dr Heinz Kiosk, the eminent social psychologist and chief psychiatric adviser to the Meringue and Profiterole Authority, comments: "It is unlikely to be the only one for long. What were these youths' attacks on the library but a cry for help? What were their bricks and other missiles but an attempt to make a statement profoundly relevant to our unjust, consumerised society, a statement we ignore at our peril?

"To the deprived underclass to which these young people belong, the library, with its books and other class-orientated artefacts and its militaristic defences, represented nothing less than a 'fortress' of reactionary elitism hostile to their own cultural values, a fortress whose siege and reduction they saw as an urgent challenge. They took what they believed, no doubt after full discussion of the issues in a caring, democratic dialogue among themselves, was the only appropriate action.

"So long as our society, with its libraries and other oppressive symbols of the past, continues to deny the cultural values of these young people, so long will it be a guilty society. But it is not only our society which is guilty", he added, as his eyeballs began to revolve in opposite directions and he briefly levitated three feet from the ground.

"WE ARE ALL GUILTY."

Prodigy

A photograph in the *Observer* shows a small baby in the embrace of two gigantic figures of Mickey Mouse and his consort Minnie at the opening in London of what is described as "Britain's first Disney store". Are there to be more of these strange imports from America?

The baby is smiling a normal baby's normal smile. Young as he is, he seems to understand his place in the scheme of things. Yet the figures which enfold him are wearing huge plastic masks of staggering ugliness. You would expect him to shrink away in terror.

These figures — and they are only part of the great world empire of Disney — are so familiar to us that most people would have to make an effort to see what should be obvious to the normal human eye: their sheer monstrosity.

What is the meaning of this cult of ugliness in children's toys and artefacts of every kind? How has it come about that these objects, which in previous times would have seemed (however perversely fascinating) repellent and even satanic, fit only for some grotesque infernal festival, are now ordinary articles of commerce, acceptable and appealing to most people if not all?

This cult of ugliness is characteristic of an age in which everything has been turned upside down so thoroughly and successfully that we do not even notice what has happened.

Do you think I am making a great fuss about nothing, drawing portentous conclusions from harmless toys, which give pleasure to all the world? Then look again at Mickey Mouse or any product of the Disney industry and its innumerable ancillaries whose works we see on every side; look not with the eye of habit but of fresh perception, and you will know this cult of ugliness for what it is: a cult of evil. The surface of things is the heart of things.

Early Days

Last November the experts of the columnar Parakremlinological Department failed for the first time ever to produce an analysis of photographs of Soviet leaders standing on top of Lenin's mausoleum at the parade for the anniversary of the Revolution. Interpretation of the power struggle in the Kremlin had become so confused by glasnost, perestroika, yeltsinomania and other factors as to be no longer scientifically valid.

This year, if the parade takes place at all, the data are likely to be even more meagre and confusing. Minute measurements of the annual shrinkage or growth of Gorbachev's birthmark can be of little interest to anyone but parakremlinologists themselves.

A new columnar Department of Parabaghdadology and its subsidiary academic discipline Parasaddamology has been set up. I hope to give more news of its findings from time to time in non-technical language for the benefit of the layman.

A team of experts has been analysing photographs of President Saddam since the beginning of the "Gulf Crisis". Lately they have been concentrating on a photograph of his historic meeting with Mr Heath at his palace in Baghdad.

Results so far, I'm afraid, are rather disappointing. The President, seated in an armchair of outstandingly execrable design, is wearing a well-cut suit of shiny material, possibly satin, with a handkerchief just showing correctly in the breast pocket. His trousers almost certainly have turn-ups. His tie was thought at first to be Old Etonian — a sensational breakthrough! But examination by electron microscope showed it was of a plain, "quiet" colour, probably "burgundy".

The President, except for small exotic details, looks like a typical youngish retired army officer, perhaps an English golf club secretary. His slightly staring, though relaxed, expression may be the result of mild hypnosis, induced, perhaps unwittingly, by Mr Heath, who is sitting ponderously opposite him in an identical armchair.

But it is surprising that of all the strange phenomena — a bearded dwarf, for instance, peering beneath some Soviet marshal's armpit, a swift exchange of boiled sweets or fag-ends, a furtive snatch to forestall the unintentional ejection of ill-fitting false teeth — which the experts used to find regularly in the Moscow photographs there is not a trace.

The use of more sophisticated techniques — bombardment of the photograph by psi-particles or gluons in a nuclear accelerator etc. — may change the whole picture. We can only hope so. The potential value of parasaddamology in revealing the truth behind the Enigma of Baghdad and guiding Western strategy is, according to the experts, literally incalculable.

On the Ohm Farm

Scientists are trying to develop "bio-engineered" cheeses which will not merely resist but actually attack and kill the bacteria of salmonella and listeria and thus protect people from food poisoning. Down on the Ohm Farm Old Seth Roentgen, Britain's foremost scientific farmer, heard this news with a scornful laugh. "Why, bless 'ee, bor," he told a reporter, "us'n pioneered they blamed wold fightin' bacteria-killin' cheeses nigh on forty year agone".

He produced a plate with a big slice of Old Seth's Traditional Laboratory Stilton, a thick wedge of Old Seth's Genuine Old World Harvest Home Wholemeal Bread and a generous dollop of Dew-fresh Ohm Farm Butter. "Try it for thisen, lad, why don't you?" he said (he is one of the last speakers of the Genuine Old British composite dialect).

"They be arl grand bacteria-killers, tried and tested by our research scientists." This became evident when the bread, cheese and butter, not satisfied with killing their own bacteria, began attacking each other; then, as the genes implanted by bio-engineering ran out of control, swelled to monstrous size and turned on the reporter and even on Old Seth himself.

"Run for it, boyo, hoots awa', me liddle wold darlin', isn't it?" shouted the gnarled old agrotechnologist as the huge Technological Ploughman's Lunch, howling and emitting sparks, chased them through the experimental fields and forced them to take refuge in a nuclear-operated egg-sorting installation until Old Seth could call up a battery of flame-throwers on his two-way radio.

Old Voices

As Imams, mullahs, Koranic scholars and lesser luminaries met in solemn conclave in Bradford to discuss the war (on the whole they were against it), a reporter asked local Muslims their opinion of Saddam Hussein. "He should never have started it," said one elderly man. "He ought to have more sense."

Here is the authentic voice of the West Riding as it was in former times, the voice of all those elderly citizens who used to sit in bowling clubs as the rain came down, shaking their heads and slowly, portentously pronouncing on the affairs of the outer world. "They want to take that Hitler and give him a good shaking", they would say. Or, in an earlier period, "T' French — I've got no time for them, and never had."

These were the humble folk (though they did not think themselves humble, as you would soon have found: "I'm as good as you are, whoever you are — and better") who were the loyal support of Alderman Foodbotham, the 25-stone, crag-visaged, iron-watch-chained, grim-booted perpetual chairman of the Bradford City tramways and fine arts committee in the great days.

It is strange to hear the traditional voice of truculent Yorkshire common-sense coming from one who for all I know may have started life as a peasant child in Bengal or the Punjab. It is also sad. How long will that voice be heard amid the hate-filled uproar and electronic frenzy of our times?

The Great Alderman is no longer here to uphold it with his protecting care. According to legend, he did not die, but lies asleep in a convenient cave, awaiting the blast of a horn, mill-hooter or other appropriate instrument which will summon him to wake and save his city and his country in their hour of greatest need.

But the hour is late and few believe in the legend any longer.

Nature Diary

By *'Redshank'*

I see that officials of the Royal Society for the Protection of Birds have admitted overestimating the number of bitterns surviving in this country.

Instead of the 60 pairs they recorded there are only 16. The reason is that scientists taking a census of bitterns have been going from one site to another recording their mating calls without realising that the bitterns were also moving from one site to another and that they were counting the same birds several times over.

The reaction of your true countryman, himself an "endangered species" though still happily flourishing in our part of the countryside, is a hearty laugh exceeding in decibels, as the country phrase has it, the loudest boom a bittern ever gave. There's nothing he likes better than hearing of "the bird protection folk" being baffled and made to look foolish.

I have a shrewd suspicion that your "average bittern in the reed bed" will be sharing in the joke and even adding an ironical boom of his own. From my own observation the creatures of the wild strongly resent being spied on and enumerated by scientists with their whirring, buzzing boxes of electrical tricks which are only too liable to give them a nasty shock.

At the approach of scientists bitterns from our local reed bed in remote, mysterious, mist-shrouded Ascherson Mere have been known to take refuge in the bar of the Five Alls, where Old Frank the landlord, Old Jim the poacher, Old Jack the wasp-keeper, Old Zebedee the quantity surveyor, and all our other traditional "characters" hide the panic-stricken birds under their voluminous coats until the danger is past, playing "merry hell" with the statistics.

There is an old rhyme, still current in pantry and gun-room, in thatched telephone exchange and businessmen's afternoon striptease club:

"When RSPB scientists dü be near
'Tes time 'ee took evasive action, never fear".

Purple Thoughts

"Vicars Rebel over Bishop", says a headline. The bishop in question is the Rt Rev Dr Hewlett Thompson, Bishop of Exeter, present holder of the see which the great Bishop Philpotts, Tory Radical, mechanophobe, scourge of Mammon and one of the only two Anglican bishops to be tutelary heroes of this column, held 150 years ago.

In an open letter to Dr Thompson, a Plymouth clergyman accuses him of "lofty disdain"; the hierarchy in general, he says, is "cocooned and complacent ... separated from the real world by chauffeurs, secretaries and gardeners". Other clergymen of the diocese complain of "demigods" and "purple bureaucrats".

If only it were so! How much more hopeful would be the outlook for the Church of England if lofty disdain were the attitude of all its bishops from Canterbury downwards, rather than apologetic mumbling, slack-jawed grovelling to the whims of the vulgar too-many and miserable attempts to join them in their low-minded amusements!

The frown of a Bishop of Exeter should strike terror into the hearts of the lower clergy as he processes in a blaze of purple through the streets to his cathedral, a majestic figure in full canonicals, accompanied by a throng of secretaries, gardeners, treasurers, archivists, messengers and beadles brandishing iron-tipped staves.

Even his numerous chauffeurs, taking their allotted turns to drive his awesome, purple-gleaming Daimler, wear a permanent haughty sneer of superiority, as the cowed multitudes of his flock part before the caval-cade, shading their eyes, and sink to their knees in holy dread.

He enters through the richly-carved doors, and soon the sound of sacred music swells through the hushed streets, causing even members of the Chamber of Commerce to remove their hats. Now the bishop is preaching, and the ocean-boom of his tremendous voice, suffused with a lofty and just disdain, reaches even distant supermarkets, amusement arcades and local government offices, bringing home to the most igno-rant and heedless a message from another world than this.

Here is the purple not of bureaucracy but of that ancient episcopal authority which, as all thoughtful people know in their hearts, can alone renew a lost, bewildered and collapsing Church.

Provincial News

Saddam Hussein's ingenious effort to conceal his nuclear arrangements from American inspecting officers have aroused admiration in the Stretchford Conurbation. The Our Saddam Hussein Fan Club, which has been revived after closing down "for the duration" earlier this year, is recruiting thousands of new members. "You can't help admiring Our Saddam's obstinacy," says typical housewife Norma Globes, 58, of Kandahar Road, the club's general secretary.

"Anybody who remembers, as I do, having to hide homemade jam, scones and fancy pastries — or even pork pies — from enforcement officers and other nosey parkers from the Food Ministry in rationing days will salute Our Saddam's energy and determination, and wish him more power to all his elbows," she stated.

She is less happy with suggestions by militant fan club members that they should try to produce some enriched uranium themselves and send it to the Iraqi President by registered post. "Once you start meddling with nuclear physics," she says, "you never know where it will end."

But she thinks that if members of the club try to produce their own nuclear weapons, as some are talking of doing, by experimenting in their kitchens, dinettes or patio areas, it is "bound to end in tears". Moreover, the Anti-Our Saddam Hussein Fan Club, which by an ineluctable law has also been revived, would be sure to start its own experiments, "leading to a fan club nuclear arms race with consequences no woman could foresee".

"It would be just about all we needed," said Chief Superintendent J. S. Harrogate, 48, the gifted supremo of the crack Police Fan Club Squad, gloomily. "Should the fan clubs escalate from their so-called 'cultural' weapons — outsize iron-bound handbags and sawn-off stubby umbrellas — to the nuclear option, then that would be a matter of legitimate concern," he added after a pause.

Correspondence

Sir — l am sorry to see from your report of a sale of false teeth at Gotheby's that you have seen fit to give the hoary old myth of Alderman Foodbotham's "reinforced concrete false teeth" fresh currency.

As a grandson of the Great Alderman I can assure you that even if a set of reinforced concrete false teeth ever actually existed, it did not belong to him. To my own recollection his false teeth, though vast and imposing and like everything else about him exuding what I can only describe as a mystic radiance, were constructed throughout of conventional materials.

How otherwise could he have used them to such effect in the celebrated incident (see J. S. Marsden's Life, Vol.III, pp.278-311) in the Bradford council debate, in July 1912, on the proposed design by Gropius for a new tram terminus at Wibsey? To emphasise his firm opposition, he "suddenly removed his upper set and jammed it into the mahogany table. There it remained, quivering and jangling, for a good half hour, while the, Town Hall rang with its strange, portentous music."

With respect, I suggest that in future, instead of perpetuating daft, discredited stories, you check the facts, or, if incapable of that, get somebody to check them for you.
Mostyn Foodbotham,
Ilkley.

Atom Smashing Days

Britain has been invited to join a European effort to build an £800 million "atom smasher" said to be capable of "recreating conditions in the universe a fraction of a second after the 'Big Bang' of Creation". However, the United States is building a rival smasher at a cost of £4.76 billion, which makes the "European" effort look pretty pathetic.

Mr Alan Howarth, our Science Minister, believes this duplication is a waste of resources. "Competition in science is important," he says strangely, "but the world cannot afford to build in parallel.... Such issues surely deserve debate between governments."

To Paul Ohm, the noted freelance technologist whose all-technological garden at Atomdene, his Edgbaston home, is one of the Seven Wonders of the Midlands, such talk is blasphemy. "The world can never have enough atom smashers." he says. "Every country should build one according to its resources or risk becoming a laughing stock. What other point is there in existence?"

Ohm has built a small atom smasher of his own, and is going ahead with his experiments no matter what Britain, Europe, the United States, Zambia, Gombola or Burkina Faso may do. He claims to have already recreated conditions in the universe 2 hours, 43 minutes and 15 seconds BST after the "Big Bang" and to be "narrowing the gap".

Cheryl Toast, the 20-year old former trainee air hostess who has somehow attached herself to Ohm in spite of his remonstrances, is, though well-meaning, small help in his work. The other morning, while he was busy smashing atoms, she suddenly cried: "Look, Paul, I've found a blade of grass. Isn't it lovely?"

Every trace of vegetation is excluded from Ohm's all-technological garden. Leaving his atoms to smash themselves, he stormed out, stamping furiously on the offending grass and shouting, "Go Away! Can't you see I'm busy?" As Cheryl sadly tried to comfort herself by assuming a bright, mechanical smile and going through the motions of the standard airline safety procedure, Ohm smashed back to his apparatus to find that several million years had been lost in a few seconds and creation was further off than ever.

Triad

Three things to avoid: A druid wearing co-respondent shoes: a prince's mead-hall with underfloor heating: a Welsh translation of *The Satanic*

Verses — from the Grey Book of Glynsabon.

Extremism

"Proportional representation," said Mr Baker, the Home Secretary, towards the end of the election campaign, "has helped the fascists to march again in Europe. It is a terrible warning to us about what could happen if we threw away our system of first-past-the-post elections."

Objectionable and un-English as proportional representation is, sponsored, moreover, by the "Europe"-crazed "Paddy" Ashdown and his Liberal Democrats, Baker's outburst yet seems frenetic and nonsensical. The people who voted for what are called "extremist" and "fascist" parties in France and Germany seem to have mostly done so, however mistakenly, for one reason only: fear that the stability of their countries is threatened by unassimilable immigrants and bogus "asylum-seekers". They are not so much "on the march" — where are their jackboots, eagle emblems and other traditional paraphernalia? — as shambling along in worry or despair.

In this country, which has no serious experience of genuine fascism, the word "fascist" is beginning to be applied to anyone who does not accept the statutory myth of the "multi-racial society", imposed on us by successive governments, who have even contrived to make any open, honest discussion of it illegal.

By the Great Semantic Shift which has operated in English politics over the past 30 years or so, opinions on this and many other matters which were once held by the majority and described as "moderate", "of the centre" or merely "patriotic" have gradually come to be described first as "right-wing", then as "extreme right-wing", then as "lunatic fringe" and finally as "fascist".

It is possible, however, that such once commonsensical opinions are still held by many, perhaps most people in this country, even though they are afraid to say so. No wonder politicians of all parties are terrified that these opinions and feelings might find open expression through elected members of parliament. Their own consensual efforts to deny and suppress them would then be exposed for the deceitful sham they have always been.

If this should happen, and the long-suppressed voice of moderate, long-suffering English people should be heard at last, that voice might well be captured, taken over and perverted by genuine "extremists" and "fascists" for abhorrent and evil purposes. Who would be most to blame but those who have so long suppressed it?

Eternal Shame

Politicians of the two parties defeated at the 1992 general election have been agonising over their defeat. "It was a choice," explains Mr Kinnock, "between hope and fear, and fear was what won out." Mr Ashdown, hoping for success in the council elections, says: "I have a vision of the people of Britain going to the polling booths on April 9 with their coat collars turned up, furtively to vote for the Conservatives. I think they will now allow themselves to cast the votes they really wanted to cast and couldn't for fear of Labour."

But will this be enough to purge the overwhelming guilt, shame and remorse which most of those who voted Conservative are now feeling? There are some of course, like myself, hard of face and hard of heart, wedded to greed and crass materialism, glad to share in the satisfying work of oppressing the poor and homeless. Far from feeling sorry, we are absolutely delighted.

But for the majority it is different. Do we realise the sheer volume of anguish these remorseful voters are now feeling?

They weep not only in private in their beastly little smug suburban homes; worse, even in public they suddenly give way to an uncontrollable grief their still turned up coat collars cannot conceal. Even the rainy skies seem to share their pain. Nature herself feels guilty over Kinnock and Ashdown.

All over the country psychotherapists and workers in the counselling industry report a flood of new patients. Many are haunted by shame-ridden memories of Kinnock in the days, so cruelly brief, of his hope and glory, punching the air and grinning like an exploding fruit-machine; or of Ashdown, his face positively racked with sincerity, his piercing eyes manfully narrowed as they search the furthest horizons of liberal democracy.

"How could I do this to them? How could I so wantonly spoil their happiness? All they wanted, after all, was a little innocent power and public attention, and I, out of selfish fear have snatched it from them! How can I ever atone for what I have done?"

The therapist listens. But somehow it seems pathetically inadequate to comfort a poor, hollow-eyed wretch whose wasted cheeks are marked by the burning fever-spots of quenchless guilt by just advising him to vote Liberal Democrat at the council elections.

What then will suffice? Surrender of all his worldly goods, a life devoted to the poor? An individual barefoot peace mission to Afghanistan or Bosnia?

Dr Heinz Kiosk, the eminent social psychologist and chief psychiatric adviser to the National Meringue and Profiterole Council, has called for a massive government-funded programme of counselling for everybody.

"Not only are Conservative voters guilty," he told a conference of experts at Droitwich yesterday. "But" — too late they began clambering over chairs and fighting for the exits as he bawled in triumph: "WE ARE ALL GUILTY!"

Things to Come

Ever searching for fashionable issues and received opinions, the Archbishop of Canterbury has turned his attention to the "global environmental crisis", the "population explosion" and the programme for universal contraception to be peddled at the forthcoming "United Nations Earth Summit", a gathering of expensive verbalisers whose very name guarantees a stupendous fraudulence.

Dr Carey is appealing to the Pope to change the Catholic Church's doctrinal opposition to contraception. But this, far from being an arbitrary piece of reactionary cussedness, as the gullible and foolish have been led to believe, is based on subtle and profound arguments about the true nature of human life.

It stands against the relentless advance of the "contraceptive mentality" which seeks to apply the attitudes and methods of the scientific laboratory to the most intimate relations of human beings. Since Dr Carey says he "doesn't fully understand the Roman Catholic position", perhaps the Pope will try to explain it to him in simple language.

Parroting statistics with the best, Dr Carey says the population of the world will rise by 97 million a year until the end of the decade and double by the middle of the 21st century; 90 per cent of this increase will be in the "Third World".

This warning depends on the belief that it is possible to predict the future. Though it comes in the guise of pseudo-science, it is no more to be trusted than its ancient equivalents, divination by eggshells or by the flight of birds. It is possible, even likely, that the population of the world, far from increasing in the next decade, may be reduced by war, plague and other disasters by half or a quarter or even to virtually nothing.

Yet on the basis of pseudo-scientific divination Dr Carey and those who think like him (that is to say, all supposedly "reasonable" people) want to sacrifice the real present to a conjectural future, to control countless millions of people, mostly the helpless people of the "Third World", to transform their manners and customs and turn their lives upside down.

This will not be done, in effect, to feed them or make them happier or healthier but to make them conform, whether by threats or cajolements, to the practices which, with all their attendant evils, are already rotting and perverting the natural instincts in our "developed world".

Some may think it the duty of an archbishop, rather than promoting projects of secular social engineering for the sake of a "New World Order", to attend to his own true concerns: supernatural evil; Satan loose in the world; the Wrath to Come. At any rate, this would make a change from opinions we can hear daily from any collection of professional gabblers, from the cheap cliché-managers of our own "media" to the luxurious windbags of the United Nations.

Higher Education

Now that polytechnics have become universities and vice versa (have I got this right?), it has become difficult to find university titles for them all. Some polytechnics, for example those of Leeds, Manchester, Nottingham, Sheffield and Oxford, are disputing with neighbouring universities, which already have the names they want.

Nowhere is the argument fiercer than in the Stretchford conurbation. It has three post-war universities, Stretchford, Nerdley and Soup Hales ("the big three") which in the great days of student demonstrations often combined forces and were a byword for Left-wing ferocity.

Ken Slabb, 26th-year sociology student, perpetual president of the students' representative council and de facto commander-in-chief of the joint demonstrational forces of the three universities, believes they should simply absorb the polytechnics which have the same names. This would increase their demonstrational strength by as much as three or four divisions — untrained levies now, perhaps, but capable of being licked into shape for the great anti-racist street battles to come.

There are also dozens of universities in Stretchford's picturesque University Quarter in Canal Road, promoted by the council's dynamic Tourism Department as a prime attraction. One of the oldest (founded 1975), richest and most successful is the Independent University of St Oick, named after the Apostle of Stretchford (fl. 600), famous for his defiance of the wicked heathen King Penda of Mercia and for the unusual wall-to wall carpeting and early Saxon central heating system of his forest hermitage.

The Chancellor, Dr Ron Plantagenet, reckons to confer about 300 honorary degrees a day, or 500 in the summer, when crowds of tourists, inflamed by colourful brochures, come to take photographs and hand over their money for impressive-looking parchment scrolls, academic gowns with hoods in "the colours of your choice — also available in tartan — please specify clan required", and "genuine gold-colour" mortarboards. St Oick is unique in the University Quarter in having a whole semi-detached house to itself. Some of the houses in Canal Road contain a dozen universities, and in one, No 47, as you go towards the Star of Bangladesh Imperial Curry Institute in Lampton Bridge Road, there are six universities in one small attic room.

There is fierce competition among them all and brawls — advertised by the Tourist Department as "a traditional feature of university life going back to the mist-ridden bogs of the Middle Ages" are an added attraction. A free-for-all among all the universities and polytechnics as they demand names of their own will make them even more of a draw.

Earthbound

Not To be outdone by parvenu Rio de Janeiro, the age-old Stretchford Conurbation has staged its own "Earth Summit". Speaking at an inaugural banquet in the gigantic Civic Centre, whose towers pierce the clouds while sparing the ozone layer, the Chief Executive, Sir Bernard Goth-Jones, said: "We have our own special contribution to make to the great task of saving Planet Earth."

The "Earth Summit", described in a finely wrought, many-coloured, 200-page brochure as "a unique blend of ecology, heritage, tourism, biodiversity, the arts, multiracial environmentalism and global thinking", has seized the imagination of all. Even the militant housewives' fan clubs, whose continual feuding makes life in the district even more unpleasant than it would be otherwise, have found a common cause, stopping motorists to check their carbon dioxide emissions before overturning their cars and setting them on fire.

Stretchford Arts has organised dozens of exciting events, including non-stop mime, an exhibition of recycled litter at the Gnomesall Heath Arts Centre and chewed cardboard works by sculptor-in-residence Harcourt Rasp, brother of the famous ecological goal-keeper, at the old Nerdley Junction Railway Subsidence Museum.

Marylou Ogreburg's Multiracial Bread and Marmite People's Street Dance Theatre is putting on a special show, "A Cry for Help from Planet Earth", likely to be echoed by householders along the way as they cower behind barred doors, trying to comfort their screaming children and whimpering rottweilers.

Dr Llewelyn Goth-Jones, the dynamic director of community medicine, who like most prominent Stretchford people is related to the Chief Executive, has put on a condom exhibition in aid of the campaign against the "population explosion". It is sponsored by Malebolge Chemicals, the pharmaceutical division of the Nadirco Consortium, of which Dr Goth-Jones is a director.

The Aztec community in Nerdley is held up as an example to all for promoting the ecological values of pre-Columbian America in face of the evil European exploiters of Planet Earth. *Aztec Heritage*, the bestseller by Royston Huitzilopochtli, the Aztec leader, and Gillian Paste of GPI Television, is to be dramatised as a 21-part television series.

But plans to stage a human sacrifice, with a Tory councillor as chief victim in place of Harold Pinter, who has not yet replied to the Aztecs' invitation, are held up by legal difficulties, described by the Labour Councillor Don Binliner as "sheer neo-Nazism".

The high point of the Summit was to have been a million-strong rock festival, with Earthrock, the ecological heavy anti-metal group, and a galaxy of stars including Jerk Avalanche, Stench Crevasse of the Spirochaetes and the veteran teenage idol Ron Frabb, Stretchford's greatest son, recently given the freedom of the city.

A small token rainforest had been brought from the Amazon and transplanted in lovely, sex-maniac-haunted Sadcake Park, where the Festival was to take place. But the environment-crazed organizers had reckoned without Mr R. D. Viswaswami, thought to be the only naked sadhu in this country, who is employed by the Council to live in a hermit's grotto of artificial stone on the island in the boating lake.

As the infernal uproar began, a vile subhuman howling backed by pounding rhythm, and the packed devotees began to wave their pallid tentacles, the indignant sadhu suddenly projected one of those "Tibetan-type" thought-forms in which he is adept. It was one of his very biggest and best.

A genuine rainforest, dark, steaming, immense, infested with poisonous snakes and insects and fetid man-eating flowers, seemed to close down around the now struggling, cursing mob. But piercing their cries of hate and fear, as they fled confusedly from the park, could be heard (was it part of the holy man's projected thought?) a single, pure, crystalline note of triumph.

Pest

The Ramblers' Association, though not one of the most dangerous pests

in this country, is certainly one of the most irritating. It has just made
another bid for notice by publishing a "list of shame" of landowners and
farmers who block up footpaths it claims are rights of way. Some of
these are disused paths, which nobody except members of the Ramblers'
Association has the slightest wish to use. Even when the owners offer to
re-route them in a more convenient way, the Ramblers reject this on
principle.

This proves, if proof were needed, that their campaigns are partly
political, an attack on the principle of private property, the very foundation of human freedom. The language they use in their windbagging
pronouncements attests this clearly.

David Beskine, described as an officer of the Association, says:
"Landowners' leaders praise the path network, but thousands of farmers
and landowners regularly plough up, plant over or otherwise obstruct
public footpaths. The Ramblers' Association is brimming over with dedicated footpath fighters who are determined to get all public footpaths
reopened." Landowners' leaders! Footpath fighters! This is the familiar
old rant, stale but unmistakable, of Leftist agitprop.

A woman described as a "county official" of the Association (how
many thousands of officials has it got, for heaven's sake?) complains
that a golf course has been built on a long-distance path so that "if you
want to follow the Oxfordshire Way you walk through the clubhouse
and are given a hard hat to go through the basement, up a flight of stairs,
on to the ground floor and out again".

How dull and unimaginative these people must be! Can't they just
enjoy the sheer strangeness of this experience? It offers a poetic vision
of the real "English countryside" as it now is, a weird, "post-modern"
jumble of disparate elements. If there were a fierce bull waiting for the
ramblers outside the clubhouse, with a stone circle full of fertiliser bags,
a group of cooling towers gently fuming in the distance and a few unsea-
sonable snowflakes drifting down, it would be perfect.

People and Parties

A new biography of Lady Ottoline Morrell, the renowned châtelaine of
Garsington Manor, (whines Rex Hickfield) suggests, on the evidence of
recently discovered journals, that her affair with a young stonemason
may have provided the idea for *Lady Chatterley's Lover*.

Scenting a mystery, I dropped in at the roomy Kensington flat where
my old friend Connie Mellors (Lady Chatterley that was) lives with her
ex-gamekeeper, popular nature-film writer and TV personality Oliver.

Over a glass of Cyprus sherry ("all we can afford nowadays," she sighed
— but did I glimpse some superior sherry on a nearby shelf?) we chatted
easily about old times.

"Ottoline? Of course I remember her." A momentary frown appeared
on her fine brow beneath the still abundant hair with its almost imperceptible blue rinse. At 85, Connie is still a strikingly beautiful woman.
"I think it was at Garsington that I first met Bert Lawrence — D. H.
Lawrence, you know. But I can't imagine Ottoline having an affair with
a stonemason. In those days the working class still had, well, certain
standards. And poor Ottoline...."

She laughed mischievously. "No, it was Bertie Russell, poor fellow,
who took up with her. He'd just made a ludicrous, of course unsuccess-
ful pass — is that the right expression nowadays? — one does get so out
of touch — at *me*. He could be dreadfully tiresome, you know. And
Ottoline, typically, got him on the rebound.

"Of course there were jealous scenes with Mark Gertler and Lytton
and Carrington and Bert Lawrence himself and, I think. Whistler and
Alma Mahler and — oh, it all seems such a long time ago." A look of
panic had come over her fine-boned face and perhaps it was as well that
just then there was a tremendous crash in the study next door.

Next moment Oliver Mellors strode in, at 90 still erect and handsome in his well-cut, well-worn tweeds. He was furious. "Look here.
Connie," he shouted. "If I could get my hands on those little pipsqueaks
at the BBC, I'd — do you realise they've dropped my series *Woodland
Kids* from the nature slot in the BBC2 afternoon schedule? And..."

Suddenly catching sight of me, he blushed painfully. "Er — dunnot
thee worrit, Connie, little lass. Me an' thou, we'll see this through together,"
"Oliver," said Connie nastily, "you really don't have to talk in that ridiculous
way any more...." Sensing marital discord, I dropped out.

Hear All Sides

The GPI Television Network's discussion programme on women's ordination in its *Hear All Sides* series was well received by all the critics
who matter. ("Brilliant and admirably balanced" — Pippa Dreadberg,
Sunday Progressive). It was certainly in the best traditions of the GPI.

Taking part were Dr "Ed" Spacely-Trellis, Bishop of Bevindon;
Giselle de Frabazon, actress and television personality; Deaconess
Mantissa Shout of St Ecumena's Church, Soup Hales; Catholic theolo-
gian Sean MacGuffog, formerly of the IRA; black feminist novelist
Leroyina Smith, tipped as a future Booker Prize winner; Dr Pixie Dutt-

Pauker, head of the department of social protestology at Stretchford University; and 88-year-old retired vicar the Rev Norman Sheep-Harris, who has recently undergone an educational course of electroconvulsive therapy for senile depression at St Bogwena's Hospital, Nerdley.

Dr Trellis and most of the other speakers agreed that to deny women ordination on the same terms as men was a manifest absurdity, contradicting the accepted principles of sex equality; it was a question of social justice and of setting an example to the Third World.

When Mr Sheep-Harris, "with the greatest respect, if I may", tried to say, in a quavering, almost inaudible voice, that "there might perhaps be a case, might I say, for the more traditional view held by some Anglican communicants", the others rounded on him furiously. Leroyina daringly spat on his bald head and MacGuffog controversially produced a rusty machine-gun from under his habit and threatened him with it, making him shrink back in his seat amid general amusement.

GPI, anticipating what Sir Godfrey Fobster, its genial, unpopular chairman, has called "stale, knee-jerk allegations of Left-wing bias from clapped-out old Tories and idiot Blimps", had arranged for Mr Sheep-Harris to put his eccentric minority view in a two-minute broadcast at 12.30 am. But he did not feel quite up to it and had to return to hospital. So a reading from her autobiography by Deaconess Shout was broadcast instead ("profoundly moving" — Pippa Dreadburg).

Nature Diary

By '*Redshank*'

As I peer through my study window at the incessant rain and listen to the howling gale, I reflect thankfully that even this weather has its compensations for those with eyes to see. I never cease to marvel how the creatures of the wild use every resource in their battle for survival.

The last leaves have fallen from the trees of Fawsley Wood. But here and there small groups of dotterel can be seen collecting bunches of leaves and trying to put them back on the bare boughs. These idiosyncratic birds, still common in our part of the countryside, do this every winter in an attempt to conceal their nests from prying eyes. But as the old country saying has it, "their success rate is minus zero".

Looking through my field glasses one morning, I noticed that a party of "sales reps", as the country folk term them, had put up a baize-topped folding card-table in a glade and were engaged in their traditional game of solo whist. They are hardy folk, these reps, and in spite of the pouring rain disdained umbrellas. As I watched, I saw them manfully handling the cards and puffing at disintegrating cigarettes, some smoking several at once.

But tempers were running short. An exultant cry of "abundance!" came faintly to my ears. The caller's triumph was short-lived. One of the other players stood up, cramming his old-fashioned trilby hat far down on his own head with an indignant gesture, and then, gathering up his sodden cards, slowly forced them down his opponent's neck. "Suddenly all hell broke loose," as the country folk say, as a mighty gust of wind whirled all the remaining cards off the table.

Would the disgruntled reps, I wondered, seek solace at the Bull and Trumpet down in the village? When I called there later on, I found no sign of the card-players except for a big salesman's order book which Old Matt the Beekeeper was meditatively chewing as he sat in his personal inglenook by the fire, occasionally squinting meaningly up the chimney.

My inquiries met with blank stares and a slow, concerted nodding from Old Frank, Old Jim, Old Fred, Old Marzipan and the other "regulars", with a counterpoint of his own transverse nods from Old Jack the landlord. Even today the ways of your true countryman survive in all their ancient inscrutability, I reflected, as I took my leave, and the wind, as though reading their immemorial thoughts, promptly blew me sideways into a flooded ditch.

Epic Encounter

Breaking a self-imposed rule, I watched a television programme about the Serbian Epic Tradition. One good reason for watching it was that members of a group called Action on Bosnia had tried to have it suppressed. These people, who included a reader in "peace studies" at Bradford University, objected to Radovan Karadzic, leader of the Bosnian Serbs, being described as a poet.

They managed to get the preamble of the programme amended so as to say "thinks of himself as a poet", with an explanation that "the peasant tradition of epic verse which has survived since the Middle Ages, combined with an irrational view of history, has helped to fuel the horrific conflict in what was once Yugoslavia". Karadzic cannot be a poet, they think, because he is on the wrong side.

But is the Bosnian Serbs' view of history more truly irrational than that of readers in peace studies? Their history since the Middle Ages (subjection to the Turks, resistance, eventual liberation) is at least their own real history, not a bloodless international abstraction. As for Mr

Karadzic, he is quite as entitled to think of himself as a poet as, for example, Stephen Spender.

He is a descendant of Vuk Karadzic (1787-1864), who as everybody knows was a noted Serbian patriot and collector of folk poetry and is regarded as the founder of the modern Serbian literary language. The present Mr Karadzic, a big tousle-headed man with a romantic air of being at ease with extreme violence, has just had the honour of being named as a "war criminal" by humbugging American politicians speaking in the name of "the international community".

He was seen in the programme smiling ambiguously among his fellow warriors, shyly reciting one of his own poems and playing the *gusle*, an elaborately carved one-stringed fiddle. His people were taking part in ceremonies, religious and secular, commemorating their irrational history, baptising their children in the waters of Kosovo, scene of their defeat by the irrational Turks in 1389 and symbol of Serbian nationhood, and dancing, men and women together, their traditional dances, with the stunningly beautiful pastoral landscape of Bosnia around them suffused with golden, irrational light.

It was just like any old BBC programme about exotic peasant culture, except that the peasants were heavily armed and ready to let off their guns at any moment. Below their pure mountain heights could be seen the hideous proletarian tower blocks of that Marxist-industrial Sarajevo they claim as theirs. A peasant culture; but instantly falsified by the fact of being filmed.

No wonder these Bosnian Serbs were described elsewhere in the programme as "the most hated people in the world". No wonder "the international community", that fraudulent abstraction so dear to progressive thinkers and projectors of a New World Order, is inimical to them. No wonder the proponents of peace studies would like to wipe them violently off the face of the earth.

They stand not only for savage crimes but also for old-fashioned concepts like martial glory, honour, loyalty, ancestral memory, pride of race and other such wicked things: awkward irrational survivals which must be eliminated if the New World Order, banal, liberal, hedonistic, is to come to power — and a good thing too, most people in the West will say.

What hope is there for their romantic stance? Made over, as they were here, into an electronic peep-show, they might have thought despairingly of a final gesture of irrational defiance — turning their guns first against the cameras remorselessly incorporating them into the modern world which hates them; and then against themselves.

Relevant, Meaningful

"Danger, of the most literal kind, gives the show its starting point," writes an art critic in an enthusiastic notice of Gravity and Grace, an exhibition of modern sculpture at the Hayward Gallery. "The first space is dominated by Richard Serra's *Five Plates, Two Poles*, a rusted steel colossus which threatens to keel over and crush anyone rash enough to touch it. Closer inspection reveals that the heavy leaning plates are all securely lodged in the poles traversing the floor."

This is feeble, timid, derivative stuff. In the real world it is 30 years and more since notices of the work of the Nerdley-born sculptor Jan Ghastbin (né Gasby) appeared in this column. Ghastbin's huge open-air rubbish-sculptures, first exhibited at the Nerdley Municipal Waste Disposal Unit One Gallery, did not just threaten to fall on people who came near them; they fell on them and engulfed them without more ado.

One rapt critic who came too close was dragged inside and imprisoned. But he still kept on talking about the work's "stunning tactile values combined with a brooding subversive humour operating on many levels and informed by an essentially tangential force in which elements of sporadism merge with wry lyricism in a vast, satisfying linear soup" until he was stifled and silenced by a mass of stale cake, one of the primal elements of this epoch-making work.

In his later oeuvre, Ghastbin concentrated on smaller "pared down, austere, neo-minimalist" works incorporating iron bars which shot out and knocked people unconscious if they came too near. His "sculpture sequences", *Controlled Explosions*, wrecked several galleries in an assertion of complex, significantly offensive integrity challenging facile preconceptions of aesthetic categories even when buried under piles of rubble" (Gandomar Fork: *An Introduction to Jan Ghastbin*; Viper and Bugloss, £85).

If Only

"The way we handle the Bosnian situation may decide whether the US and Europe move forward to the 21st century or backwards to the 19th," says the American Senator William Cohen. If only we had the choice! Who in his senses, whether in Europe or America, would not rather move backwards to the 19th century than forward to the 21st?

In the 19th century the world-wide domination of Europe was still assured, while the United States, though already growing overmighty, was still busy sorting out its own problems and, on the whole, minding its own business in a commendable way.

The civilisation of Europe, the greatest civilisation in the history of the world, was still intact. The British Empire was playing its beneficent part in the world, maintaining the freedom of the seas and, with its much-appreciated dominion over palm and pine, guarding the interests of peoples scarcely capable of looking after themselves. There was no Bosnian situation which could not be dealt with by agreement between the great European powers (it was, of course, because this agreement broke down in the 20th century that a Bosnian situation arose which by a malign series of events wrecked the whole show).

But American senators and other politicians of today, just like those who by interfering in Europe earlier in the century for the sake of "self-determination" helped to ensure that the Bosnian situation would persist indefinitely, do not seem to know much history.

Senator Cohen sees the 21st century as the century in which a New World Order or World Government will at last come into being as the crown and consummation of all the ages, the permanent safeguard of peace, democracy and world-wide mass-culture in which outmoded little local loyalties and traditions, whether those of the Serbs or anybody else, will be eliminated for the good of all.

But what to the senator seems a self-evident good may seem to others the worst of nightmares, the rule of the lowest common denominator, a system of tyranny more fearful and oppressive than any known to history, because it would be universal and therefore immovable, unassailable and without appeal. If that is to be the 21st century, it would even be better, since sadly we cannot get back to the 19th, to stick with the 20th as long as we can manage to do so.

Is This Your Problem?

By Claire Howitzer

Dear Claire Howitzer: I am 25, 18-stone, with a variegated complexion, receding hairline and large outstanding ears. I am considered quite attractive and intelligent (I have a degree in non-smoking studies from Soup Hales University). I work in an office where my men and women colleagues all seem to be seriously in need of having their consciousness raised regarding women's rights and the problem of sexual harassment and rape.

Although I have made my own attitude clear, none of my colleagues has ever tried to sexually harass me either by touching, pinching, stroking, groping, telling suggestive jokes or other statutory methods of harassment as laid down in my women's rights manual. These men and women seem to get on quite well with each other, to judge from the bursts of laughter I often hear. I suppose they must be telling each other suggestive jokes, but I am glad to say I cannot understand them.

If things go on like this I see little or no hope of bringing a charge of sexual harassment, let alone rape, against any of them. Yesterday I was looking hard at one man, who is particularly inclined to joke with the other women and ignore me, as I had some idea of raising his consciousness. After a while he seemed to notice me. Then he suddenly went pale and slumped to the ground unconscious.

What ought I to do in order to get sexually harassed and perhaps be able to bring a charge of rape against somebody, as most women of my age seem to be doing? (Beth Truck. Nerdley.)

Claire Howitzer replies: This is still a problem, Beth, for a lot of working women nowadays, even though the idea of sexual harassment for everybody is making steady and heartening progress. Have you thought of changing your job? How would you feel about joining the police force?

From what I hear, it has become a very promising field for asserting women's rights. A recent survey showed that out of 1,800 policewomen surveyed, 48 per cent said they had been touched, stroked or pinched by fellow officers, and 92 per cent had heard suggestive jokes.

If you became a policewoman, I can't promise you would actually be harassed or raped, but at least you might have a good chance of making an accusation of rape or harassment. If the police refuse to accept you as a recruit, please write to me again, as you might be able to bring a complaint of unfair discrimination before the Equal Opportunities Commission.

A Fine Example

There are reports from Bradford of growing discrimination against the large "ethnic communities" in the city. As in all such cases, most people will ask themselves: what would be the attitude of Alderman Foodbotham, the 25-stone crag-visaged, iron-watch-chained, grim-booted perpetual chairman of the Bradford City Tramways and Fine Arts Committee, for many years Lord Mayor?

Foodbotham was entirely without racial prejudice. A consciousness of his own unblemished West Riding descent through uncounted generations from the chieftains of Deira onwards, to say nothing of his own unmistakable personal superiority, placed him above such petty feelings. That there might be foreigners in Bradford, even a few coloured people, he readily admitted. But provided they never ventured to enter the Town Hall or otherwise intrude into his majestic orbit, he took, in his own accustomed phrase, "no cognisance" of them.

His attitude is well documented in J. S. Marsden's standard five-volume Life. For example, among the innumerable gifts he received from all parts of the world on the 10th anniversary of his Lord Mayoralty in 1923 was a ceremonial elephant, richly caparisoned in gold and jewels, from the Maharaja of Shakrapur, an old admirer. It was accompanied by two mahouts, Muslims from East Bengal (or "Bangladesh" as it is now called).

The elephant was housed in one of the ceremonial tramsheds at Green Garth, the alderman's titanic mansion on Cleckheaton Moor. An attempt to introduce it into a procession as part of the celebrations was rather a fiasco. It got wedged between two flower-decorated trams, and one of the mahouts panicked when he got a minor electric shock from a displaced overhead conductor rail. But it never entered Foodbotham's head to criticise either the elephant or the mahouts.

Although their ceremonial role had to be abandoned, they stayed on at Green Garth for many years and were treated with great consideration. The elephant became a great favourite with visitors. As for the mahouts, the great alderman made a point of providing living accommodation in a remote part of his park by no means inferior to what they might have expected in their native Bengal.

He even ordered a small two-man mosque to be built for them, and engaged an imam and a muezzin out of the Public Baths Department funds. When certain disaffected council officials whined about "waste of public money", he issued a contemptuous glare which soon had them grovelling on their knees, and, had he not magnanimously prevented them, they would literally have licked his awesome boots.

To quote Marsden, "the calling of the two faithful to evening prayer, sounding mysteriously through the cedar-infested domains, mingling with the howling of the wind and the strains of the alderman's personal tramwaymen's brass band, could be heard distinctly above the traffic in the city centre, bringing home even to the dull of soul that in this world things are not always precisely what they seem."

The alderman's unfailing kindness to these exotic creatures so far from home might be quoted today as a fine example of "race relations" at their best. But I doubt it will be. Some people are never satisfied.

Gigs Tonight

Poisoned Meringue. Epidemiological Rap. With Bo Anthrax and the
Botules. Old Phosgene Storerooms, London SW19. 8pm. £15 admission.

The Qualtroughs. Manx Rock. Plus the Snaefell Bassoonettes and
Alan Cake. London Celtophone Centre. 9pm. £10.

Exploding Clavichord. 18th century Punk Rock. Dave Necker and
the Antoinettes. Brassgrove Park Underpass SW90. 9pm. £15.

Anna Comnena and the Basils. Byzantine Rock. Palaeologue Rooms
SW7. 10pm. Court Dress only. £1,500.

Sporting Chances

Senior figures in the Church of England, the *Observer* reports, are worried that bishops may be caught up in an "unseemly race" to be the first
to ordain a woman priest. "With more than a dozen bishops already pencilling in dates ... an undignified scramble may be inevitable if legislation on women priests clears its final hurdle," says the article, flogging
the sporting imagery a bit.

Legislation is likely to be passed in Parliament this autumn and the
"final hurdle" will be a special meeting of the General Synod of February 22. The genial, fatheaded Bishop of Durham, Dr David Jenkins, has
already pencilled in May 28 and 29 for the ordination of about 40 women
in his cathedral. Dr Stephen Sykes, Bishop of Ely, is level pegging. But
the bishop most fancied to be first past the post is Dr Philip Goodrich of
Worcester, who hopes to ordain about 20 women a fortnight before them.

Alas for all their hopes! Dr Spaceley-Trellis, the go-ahead Bishop of
Bevindon, can afford to laugh. "It'll be a doddle," he keeps on telling his
domestic chaplain, the Rev Peter Nordwestdeutscher, who winces painfully every time at his master's fondness for colloquialisms, especially
rather dated ones.

Dr Trellis has already lined up more than 3,000 women for ordination, and they will be under starter's orders the moment the balloon goes
up on February 22. In accordance with his ecumenical principles, which
as he says, deftly switching to his "public" mode, "are essential if we are
to build a church with appeal for the average woman and man in our
secular day and age in a very real sense", his new women priests will be
a mixed lot. Among them are well-known militant feminists like Deaconess Mantissa Shout and Deaconess Schulamith Fischbein, daughter

of the eminent psychologist and TV erotician Dr Melisande Fischbein. But there are also representatives of progressive groups in the Stretchford Conurbation, which is in the Bevindon diocese. There are many social workers, child-abuse experts, environmental health workers including members of the anti-smoking community, professional anti-racists, "right to choose" pro-abortion campaigners and other experts in consciousness-raising.

In the interests of ecumenism, Dr Trellis has included as many women with non-Christian connections as possible. There are Buddhists (plain and tantric), New Age witches, soothsayers and worshippers of the Great Green Earth Mother. There are several women from the Inner Nerdley Aztec community, where a breakaway radical feminist sect is claiming the right to perform ceremonies of human sacrifice hitherto reserved for male priests.

"For the sake of our multicultural society", he would like to ordain as many Muslim women as possible. But here he has run into trouble, not only from their own people (the Chief Imam of Stretchford, Dr Iqbal Niftikarullah, has already threatened to pronounce a class-one double-ended *fatwa* against him) but also from the militant housewives' fan clubs which make life in the conurbation even more dangerous and unpleasant than it would be otherwise and, worse still, are not all entirely sound on the subject of "racism".

Ordination Day, keenly awaited by all, may turn out to resemble not so much an English sports day or point-to-point as a badly organised UN "multi-faith" women's outing in central Bosnia.

Fallen Majesty

Lights burned all night at Cavity House, London headquarters of the Amalgamated Union of Holeborers, in a traditional gesture of solidarity with delegates at the annual TUC assembly who voted for the repeal of all anti-union laws and the right to unlimited "sympathy strikes". As morning broke, a spokesman pronounced these age-old words:

"At this eleventh hour the door is still open for negotiation in a spirit of goodwill across the board at consultation and implementatory level in the context of a frank discussion-style debate, taking full cognisance of all acceptable solutions, with a long hard look at the grassroots of democratic opinion while there is still daylight at both ends of the tunnel and on the floor of the tunnel as well."

What did it matter that nobody was listening, that nobody wrote down the words or recorded them or transmitted them, as in former days, to listening millions throughout the land? What did it matter that there was nobody to switch the lights off? All is not lost.

In a remote part of the otherwise deserted building, workers in the office of Dogmatics and Rulebook Exegesis, custodians of the Rulebook and the Commentaries, the two sacred books of the union, already longer than the Bible, the Koran, the Zendavesta, the Book of Mormon and the Upanishads together, and continually growing, toiled on, coughing in solidarity amid dust and mouldering paper, at their immemorial work of collation, emendation and interpretation which will continue (Rule One) to the end of time.

Who Whom?

An experiment with a new kind of opinion poll, intended to find out what people would think if they were "better informed", is being tried out by Channel 4 Television in collaboration with the *Independent* newspaper. A representative sample of 400 people will take part in discussions with politicians, read research papers and watch television programmes about each issue before their opinions are polled.

The originator of this method is a Mr James Fishkin of the department of government at the University of Texas. He believes four out of five people hold "pseudo-opinions" on most issues rather than "informed" ones. "This is an attempt to break through the lack of understanding," he says. "The eyes of the democratic world will be on this experiment."

Whatever he may mean by the "democratic world", there is no doubt that the eyes of those who want to control and manipulate opinion will be on this experiment. Who will decide what is meant by "better informed"? Who will pick the 400 "representative people"? Who will choose the politicians they will discuss the issues with? Who will decide what research papers they read, what television programmes they watch in order to form an opinion? Who whom?

It reminds me of those old BBC programmes, invariably slanted to the Left, which were intended, we were always told, to "make people think". The sensible question to ask was: make them think what? The answer, never given, was only too obvious. What is Fishkin's experiment but a new method of liberal brainwashing?

Rather than being told what to think, in however well informed a way, people would do better to stick to their despised "pseudo-opinions". However ill informed, at least they will be their own. And in instinctive prejudices may lie true wisdom.

For Your Bookshelf

This year's edition of the *Annual Directory of Typical housewives' Fan Clubs in the Stretchford Conurbation*, out this week (Viper and Bugloss, £45), reflects the profound changes which have been coming over these clubs.

When they first began to be a menace for law, order and common sense about 30 years ago, most of them, starting with the very first, the Our Jackie Onassis Fan Club and its corollary, the Anti-Our Jackie, were devoted to various members of the Kennedy family and its in-laws, some of them quite remote and obscure like Jackie's aunt-by-marriage, Artemis Garoufalidis, unwitting patron of one of the most ferocious of all the clubs, the Our Auntie Artemis Garoufalidis, noted for its outsize ironbound handbags and distinctive bobble-fringed knitted grenade covers.

But like everything else in the world, they are becoming steadily politicised. The clubs with the biggest following are now mainly those devoted to foreign tyrants:

For example, the Our Saddam Hussein Fan Club (and, of course, the Anti-Our Saddam). Some of the most popular are the result of "creative misunderstanding": for example, the, Our Omar Yeltsin, the Our Chief Aidid Milosevic and the Our Emperor Joe Slovo Bokassa, with their various warring splinter groups.

The Directory includes specialised articles on club uniforms and insignia; notes on membership, recruiting and initiation ceremonies (the Revisionist Our Radovan Tudjman, for instance, makes would-be recruits, in a gruelling test of fitness, eat two whole cakestands-full of home-made rock buns while cutting the buttons off an outsize wine-coloured cardigan and sewing them on again in three minutes flat).

There is a full account of major incidents during the past year, including the skirmish on April 19 between elements of the Environmental Our Ali Akbar Rafsanjani and the Revisionist Our Nelson Buthelezi in the tinned cat food section of the Nadirco Hyperconsumerama in Carbon Brush Street, Soup Hales, which led to the destruction of a popular old folk's artificial ski-slope nearby.

The famous, eagerly-awaited Anonymous Preface, a controversial feature of the Directory, deals with "the social effects of the fan club movement on our multicultural democracy". Although anonymous, it is generally believed to be written by Chief Supt J. S. Harrogate, the police fan club supremo. Its air of haunting melancholy and references to pre-Raphaelite paintings and the cultivation of sunflowers certainly point in his direction.

I do not like picking holes, but there are several errors, which should not have appeared in a standard work of reference. On page 178 "Lenin" is misprinted "Lonigan"; there is no such person as Det Sgt Kenneth Humus (page 226); during the "Affair of March 23" it was Mrs Amy Smith, not Mrs Lorna Smith, as stated here, who manned the flame-thrower on the roof of the Nerdley Citizens' Charter Advisory Centre.

Splendidly Vacant

For three years after it moved to new headquarters in London, the Arts Council went on maintaining an empty annexe behind its old home. Only this month has it been able to get rid of the building, which has cost the taxpayer more than £3 million. This apparent waste of money is said to have caused consternation in the "arts world", already buzzing angrily at a likely cut of £5 million in its government grant.

Andrew Watson-Fork, *Way of the World* Art Critic, comments: "This row suggests that there are still stubborn pockets of philistinism holding out in the arts world and even in the Arts Council itself. This empty annexe, simply because of its emptiness, was itself a great work of art. Its vacancy was a powerful, deeply felt statement, adumbrating by means of total untenantedness, unblemished by the spurious concept of occupation, the void which is at the heart of everything truly creative and forward-looking in the arts today.

"This annexe showed the way forward from minimalism to the ultimate formulation of art in our time. I had the privilege of visiting it last year. I was absolutely spellbound. Here, I realised at once, was true greatness. As I walked round it, my echoing footsteps seemed to reinforce the impact of essential emptiness, bringing home to me by its breathtakingly simple, austere, blank, pared-down dynamism my own oneness with the basic void.

"What is to be the fate of this wonderful annexe, now that the Arts Council, to its eternal shame, has abandoned it? It would have been worth not £3 million but £300 million to preserve it as part of Britain's heritage. To think of it as no longer empty but containing, perhaps, mundane objects or even people is unbearable. Is it too late for the Arts Council to do its duty and apply to the Government for help to get it back?

"I am sure the art-loving public would respond generously to an appeal. I have no personal axe to grind, but to take proper care of this masterpiece as it deserves, an experienced curator with an adequate salary and resources would be essential."

A Notable Festival

Talk of a possible revival of Hammer Films may have raised similar hopes among the aged devotees of Piledriver Films, the work of that gifted director Brian Hohenzollern, whose spine-chilling productions featuring the mad philosopher Wittgenstein in heroic roles were once regularly reviewed in this column. Alas, there is no hope of a revival.

This is for two reasons: firstly, the real Wittgenstein has been formally adopted as a tutelary hero of this column; second, developments in the whole film industry, not merely in its horror department, long ago reduced Piledriver's offerings, horrific though they may once have seemed, to the status of an old-time village whist drive.

However, the fans can still look forward to the Piledriver Film Festival. Sponsored by Soup Hales Arts, this is now an annual event, held at the old Odium Cinema in Gnomesall Heath Broadway. This year's Festival, described in *Ghoul* magazine as "a rare old treat for all vintage horror film aficionados", drew greater numbers than ever. Many old favourites were screened, including Wittgenstein and the Environmental Zombies and Wittgenstein and the Social Democrats from Outer Space.

Many of the fans know the films by heart and spent the evenings arguing enjoyably about every detail. Did the radioactive grandfather clock in Furniture Depository of the Living Dead double for the man-trapping clock in the earlier Wittgenstein and the Vampire Psephologist? Was the part of the sinister fanged Carpathian innkeeper in the latter film played by Bruce Braganza or Barry Saxe-Coburg-Gotha?

Brian Hohenzollern himself introduced the Festival in a graceful speech, and several actors who were once household names put in an appearance, none looking a day older than in the time of their glory — a curious phenomenon often explained by "something in the air" of the Stretchford Conurbation.

Among them were Stan Bourbon-Parma, who used to play one of the best-loved characters, the bearded Egyptologist and explorer Sir Henry Curtis-Bennett VC; Kay Wittelsbach, Wittgenstein's beautiful violet-eyed assistant, heroine of many a hairbreadth escape from malignant dwarfs and mutant vegetables; and the veteran Sean Abdul Hamid, whose performance as a swarm of deadly asteroids in Wittgenstein and the Curse of the Zodiac will never be forgotten.

These once famous actors had to find other employment when Piledriver closed down in 1980, and life was not easy. For several years Bruce Braganza worked for GPI Television documentaries, playing White South Africans, Ulster Unionists and other statutory fiendish characters, until Nevillle Dreadberg, the producer, decided he was no longer fiendish enough. Ted Hapsburg and Bing Karageorgevitch, who wrote the hauntingly sinister music for the films, at one time worked in a Midlands factory which mass-produced new symphonies for the Mahler industry.

On the last evening of the festival there was a tremendous row between those two old rivals, Shirley Cantacuzene and Marylou Romanoff, Piledriver's chief fashion designers. Marylou, whose two sons by the historical researcher Dean Porphyrogenitus, Vlad and Brad, both emigrated to Australia and became prominent dentists, accused Shirley of keeping some of the best horror properties for herself instead of sharing them.

"She should never have had that plastic sarcophagus of Pharaoh Blothmes III," Marylou shouted, appealing to Brian Hohenzollern, "and well you know it!" "Why don't you drop dead from the Pharaoh's Curse for real?" Shirley bawled as Brian vainly tried to separate them with a plywood effigy of a radioactive werewolf.

What the Papers Say

In a thoughtful leader *Feudal Times and Reactionary Herald* discusses the agreement on a new constitution for South Africa:

"This strange but not unexpected document lays down, at the outset, the principle that 'all South Africans will be entitled to common citizenship in a sovereign and constitutional democratic state in which there is equality between men and women and people of all races so that citizens shall be able to enjoy and exercise their fundamental rights and freedoms'. Was there ever such a collection of absurdities and impossibilities gathered in so small a space?

"Citizenship, democracy, equality of race and sex, rights and freedoms — we cannot but aver that these well-worn terms, so familiar in the mouths of levellers and foaming radicals of every kind, carry little or no meaning when taken singly, and amount, when taken together, to nothing more than an horrific chimera, engendered to deceive not merely the great world but also, more cruelly, those most closely concerned, the various peoples and tribes of South Africa, whether English, Dutch, Negro or of other miscellaneous races.

"This whole phantasmagoria, in which so many false hopes have been invested, rests on the fatal principle of arithmetical democracy, universal suffrage, 'one man one vote' or by whatever other repulsive term this obfuscatory principle may be described. It is a principle which, greatly against our advice, has been imposed piecemeal on this realm over the last two centuries, with generally disastrous results.

"Here, among most responsible and reflective people, it is more and more discredited with every day that passes. With what pernicious folly, then, is it introduced into a far-off, partly savage land where it has been hitherto unknown and where nobody has demanded it save for a class of political manipulators who design to gain power over the humble and excitable many by raising hopes which cannot be fulfilled!

"These deluded wretches are to be induced, by the lure of abstract principles and by the prospect of unattainable 'rights' and 'freedoms', to forfeit whatever of humble, quotidian good they may now enjoy — for the most part of these unfortunates, we fear, little enough! They are to suffer, starve and die for a mess of fine words. Was there ever a more heartless, more wicked deception?"

Deidre's Gift

Walking along a quiet lane in Hampstead, not far from Marxmount, Mrs Dutt-Pauker's fine white mansion at the edge of the Heath, Deirdre met a black man who promptly made to snatch her handbag. But to his surprise, Deirdre handed it over before he laid hands on it. "Do please take it," she said.

"I expect you'll have heard about Bernie Grant's proposal that we white people ought to make some sort of amends for all the wrongs our ancestors did to you black people, such as the slave trade and colonialism by which we robbed you of your wealth, developed our wicked capitalist system and prevented you from developing your own rich indigenous cultures."

The man stared at her, shifting from one foot to the other and scratching his head in a worried way. His eyeballs began to revolve as she went on: "This is just a small token to show how much I agree with Bernie. Please take this batch of leaflets as well. They explain how our neocolonialist exploitation is still going on in most parts of the world. I only wish I could do more just now. Perhaps you'd let me have your name and address and 'phone number so that I..."

But the black man, whose head was beginning to buzz uncomfortably, dropped handbag and leaflets, and fled. "Oh dear," said Deirdre to herself, "I wonder what I did wrong." Ruefully picking up her property, she returned to Marxmount, where she found her mother in her study, busy with some capitalist-looking papers at her desk.

"Such an odd thing happened, Mummy. It sounds incredible, but it was as if the poor man had never even heard about Bernie Grant or colonialism or capitalist exploitation or anything."

Her mother frowned. "Perhaps you didn't explain Mr Grant's proposals in the right way. I know you meant well, but I've told you repeatedly, Deirdre, not to meddle with things you don't fully understand.

"Do go and demonstrate outside the Nicaraguan Embassy or something. I'm expecting a visit from my broker and have important matters to discuss about South Africa. Off you go, and if you meet any more black men, make sure they're members of the Labour Party."

Battles Long Ago

I'm sure I'm not the only one (writes "Old Timer") who is delighted and enthralled by the feud between two American girl ice skaters. It seems to take me back through mists of memory to my old days as a ballroom dancing fan in south London in the glamorous Fifties, when the Diane Refayne School of Ballroom Dancing still flourished and such giants as Reg Wafer, Ron Simper and, of course, the peerless Diane herself still stalked the land.

Your actual threats of violence were, of course, in short supply. Yet there were not a few moments of high drama, as passions no less intense than those "across the herring pond" seethed unutterably beneath sequinned corsage and brilliantined brains. I well remember the smouldering rivalry between that immortal duo, Reg Wafer and Diane Refayne, eight times all-England champions of the bunny-hug and Yorkshire slow waltz, and those peerless exponents of the Mexican Belota (reformed version), Ron and Elaine Simper, which at last burst into open conflagration during the 1953 Finals at the Odium Cinema Ballroom, Turgis Hill.

As the rival couples gyrated gracefully before a capacity crowd presided over by the British Ballroom Dancing Supremo Sir Dudley Honke and his fellow judges, a sensational bombshell intervened. Elaine Simper brought the proceedings to a juddering halt by loudly claiming that Reg Wafer was carrying corned beef sandwiches in his coat-tails in contravention of Rule 83B!

And so it proved. Yet Reg not only maintained that the ill-omened sandwiches of that ilk had been planted by an undercover agent working for the Simpers but counterclaimed under Rule 96 that the Simpers themselves were guilty of "grimacing horribly with the intention of distracting other competitors". A nasty altercation was only averted when the judges ruled both couples out of order and awarded the trophy to the hitherto unknown Mr and Mrs Raoul Twinge of Brassgrove Park!

As I recall, Reg and Diane and the Simpers neither forgave nor for-

got. When Ron Simper's uncle Frank, no mean ballroom dancer in his
time — for many years he captained the crack formation dancing team
of inmates from the Darby and Joan Sunset home at Soup Hales — was
gathered to his fathers in that Valhalla of Ballroom Dancing, Nerdley
Grove Cemetery, Reg and Diane were pointedly "among those not
present"!

I hope I have not taken up too much of your time.

On and On

The ludicrous controversy about the age of consent for homosexuals and
ludicrous debate in the Commons have released immense torrents of
comment in the press which are only just beginning to recede from dev-
astated minds.

One writer argues that because the Nazis held both Jews and homosexuals to be "subversive cultural influences" and persecuted both ac-
cordingly, it is therefore equally wrong for us to discriminate against
either: both are valuable minorities which by "challenging received opinion" make for progress.

He quotes George Steiner, the well-known polymath and non-stop
purveyor of high grade verbiage: "Judaism and homosexuality ... can be
seen to have been the two main generators of the entire fabric and savour
of urban modernity in the West."

This sounds like a typically glib and showy bit of generalisation. But
whether there is any truth in it or not, is it wise to talk like this? There are
plenty of people, more and more I dare say, and not all of them clerical
fascist cranks and feudal landowners like myself, who do not find "urban modernity" wholly admirable and good. To suggest that certain minorities are mainly responsible for generating it may lead to very dark
and dangerous thoughts indeed.

More Memories

"Old Timer's" memories of ballroom dancing in the Fifties have produced thousands of readers' letters, many of them stained with tears and
both alcoholic and temperance beverages. Some are written in purple
ink and badly gnawed at the edges. One anonymous reader with an address in Turgis Hill in south London sends her own scandalous reminis-
cences.

She even hints at an "ill-starred love affair" between Elaine Simper and the much venerated British Ballroom Dancing Supremo Sir Dudley Honke himself, which the writer says may have caused him to fix the contest in Elaine's favour by the use of "miracle adhesive" at the Odium Cinema Ballroom Finals in 1950. If there is any truth in this, historians of ballroom dancing, such as Harvey Gummer in his monumental three-volume Survey, will have to revise their view of this supposedly saintly figure.

One of the most interesting letters is from Mrs Yvette Twinge of Brassgrove Park, joint champion with her husband Raoul in the fateful 1953 Finals "Old Timer" wrote about. She writes: "In fairness to my late husband, who cannot defend himself in his present disadvantaged position in Brassgrove Vale Cemetary, I must point out that 'Old Timer's' so-called memories are a veritable tussore (*sic*) of lies and inaccuracies. In printing them, you have sunk to the murkiest sewers of the tabloid press.

"To kick off with — with distaste I use the only kind of language you gutter journalists understand — the so-called 'ill-omened sandwiches of that ilk' which were found in Reg Wafer's coat-tails were not corned beef as stated, but potted meat. Ron Simper's uncle Frank was not 'captain' of the formation dancing team from the Darby and Joan Sunset Home at Soup Hales (for your information they were called 'the 'Soubrettes' in honour of the Chief Matron of the Home, Mrs Nora Tanks, who had been a gifted adagio dancer with the well-known group of that name at Dankmere Haven Transit Camp during the war).

"Frank Simper, 'who or whom we knew well, was in fact training adviser to the team. Under his wise guidance it won the All-England Old Folks' Formation Dancing Trophy four years running. Lastly (for the time being), it is a travesty to describe my husband and myself as 'hitherto unknown' in 1953. As it happens, we carried off the prestigious Gold Medal for the Lancashire Two-Step at Redcar in the previous year and were photographed with Royalty and the Town Clerk of South Shields.

"I suppose it is pointless to ask you in future to verify information from such tainted sources as 'Old Timer' of that ilk before you foist it on your unsuspecting readers, if any. If you are too stupid to do this yourself, why not find somebody else who can do it for you?"

To a Fishfinger

Thou shape impacted of Old Ocean's heart,
With frost imbu'd and golden crumbs bedight,

Casual thy vending and thy worth too light:
How soon thy form symmetric must depart!
In rangéd boxes at the supermart
Thou bidest with they fellows day and night,
Nor dream'st thou'll't scale some culinary height —
Who fries and serve thee needs no subtile art!
And yet for thee the stalwart seaman rov'd
'Mid tempests' rage; and Iceland's anger keen
Endur'd; nor glimpsed 'mid perils dire the end
Sublime: that thou, scorned digit, should'st be lov'd
Dearer than pizza or th' entinnéd bean,
For soliary men both food and friend!
(From *The Oxford Book of Esperanto Verse*, edited and translated by
Julian Birdbath).

A Solemn Hush

No-Smoking Day has come and gone, with the customary ceremonies at
the Tomb of the Unknown Non-Smoker at Turgis Hill Cemetery in South
London. In a moving address, the Rev John Shrike, vicar of the local
Church of Christ the Non-Smoker, spoke of the "dangers of triumphalism.
We have got the smoker on the run, but remember, he is master of a
thousand wiles, a hundred-headed monster which grows new heads, all
smoking cigarettes, as soon as old heads are lopped off'".

He paid a special tribute to the "splendid work" of the Children's
Volunteer Units of the Anti-Smoking Liberation Front, This year, he
said, they had persuaded a record number of shopkeepers to sell them
cigarettes and then denounced them to the police, who had brought proceedings in gratifying numbers. Many of these evil shopkeepers, he was
delighted to say, had been driven out of business and some, with their
families, had been reduced to begging in the streets and living in cardboard boxes. If these were cigarette cartons, he said with an infectious
laugh, so much the better!

These junior volunteers, he went on, had also done excellent work
denouncing those of their parents who still smoked, seizing and destroying their cigarettes either by stealth or force and persuading non-smoking neighbours to shun them as they deserved.

At the subsequent parade Mr Shrike proudly commended the smart
turn-out of the children's units marching past in theit paramilitary uniforms, "magnificently keen young anti-smoking stormtroopers of the

future!"

A party from the Anti-Smoking Liberation Army, the ASLF's military wing, then fired a volley over the Tomb. A dissident group staged a demonstration to protest against the implication that it is possible to die of anything except smoking. There was also a silent vigil by members of a growing mystical sect (Non-Smokers for Eternal Life) which holds that non-smoking can actually ensure immortality.

To mark Non-Smoking Day the Visiting Professor of Non-Smoking Studies at Stretchford University, Dr E. L. Hamster, gave a lecture on "Non-Smoking, Nationalism and the United Nations", followed by readings from his new volume of autobiography, Non-Smoking My Destiny. Later there was a mass demonstration of non-smoking, creative yawning and environmental staring into space.

A Gleam of Hope

The government of Zimbabwe, as I suppose we may call Rhodesia out of politeness, has been criticised for allowing ministers and other powerful people to lease state-owned farms for themselves under its "land for all" policy instead of making them over to poor, landless peasants. The Minister for Education and Culture, the President's secretary and the chief of the Air Force are among those said to have acquired rich farmland in this way.

The Minister for Agriculture has resolutely defended his fellow members of the ruling class, arguing that they are the only people who have the money to invest in the land. "In colonial days," he says, "white people simply got a gun and told you to move off a piece of land and told you it was their farm. We do not do that."

Perhaps, they will get around to it in time, mindful of "the good old rule, the simple plan, that they should take who have the power and they should keep who can".

Improbable as it may seem, "EX AFRICA", an expert who writes on African matters in the Feudal Times and Reactionary Herald, finds a gleam of hope in this unexpected quarter.

"It may be that we are witnessing in that far-off land the first signs of a new noble caste, both black and white, which will assert once more the immemorial rights of rank and property in an unchanging, hierarchical order. Will feudal Zimbabwe — and that name, some will think, better fits the noble land we hope to see than that of the Grand Bagman and dubious adventurer after whom it was once named — prove to be a pattern and inspiration for the future world?

"Be sure that on those great estates under the burning sun, in those fine houses where custom and ceremony rule, those humble, decent villages, those fields where a secure, contented peasantry toils eternally in happy deference, there will be no place for the low-minded malcontent, the envious leveller or foaming radical   but only stern and summary justice."

Mystery Intruder

When James Pulp, alias Kevin Himmler, Wayne von dem Bach-Zalewski, Dean J. Antonescu, etc., etc., appeared at Nerdley magistrates' court charged with loitering on enclosed premises and aggravated burglary, he asked for 1,502,663 similar charges to be taken into consideration, believed to be a record for the court.

Giving evidence, Det Sgt J. S. Mackenzie, 41, of Nerdley Special Branch, said that on the morning of January 14 he was proceeding along Kandahar Road on a routine search for certain substances when he noticed the accused, who appeared, to be in a highly excited state.

He (the accused) seized him (Sgt Mackenzie) by one of the ballpoint pens in his pocket and demanded to be taken into custody. His breath smelled strongly of newsprint.

"'It says in this paper here,' accused stated, 'that unless the Scotland Yard War Crimes Unit brings some cases to court by April 1995, the Home Secretary may not be able to arrange further funding. I just want to help them out. I am a War Criminal. I don't care whether I get a fair trial or not; I just don't want to see all those millions go down the drain and nothing to show for it.'"

Sgt Mackenzie, 38, said he told Pulp he did not look old enough to have seen service in the War, either as a war criminal or anything else. Accused immediately became violent, stating that he would soon show him whether he was a war criminal or not. He (Sgt Mackenzie, 43) then arrested him.

Dr F. Gestaltvogel, 54 a consultant psychiatrist at Nerdley General Hospital, said that delusions of being a war criminal and of having personally killed millions of people were not uncommon. An eminent psychiatric colleague, Dr Heinz Kiosk, had even said "We are all war criminals." He had examined accused and, apart from an abnormally violent left patellar reflex and essential tremor up to 6-5 on the Richter Scale, he was a perfectly normal average citizen.

Mr Frank Cleary, 46, defending, asked Sgt Mackenzie, 39, how he presumed to estimate Pulp's age when his own age was notoriously subject to gross fluctuation in the band 35 to 49 and had been investigated by leading scientists as being inconsistent with current concepts of the Space-Time Continuum. But in a show of hands the board of magistrates ruled that the question was irrelevant.

Binding Pulp over, Dr Ellis Goth-Jones, the Chairman, 56, said there were puzzling aspects of the case, but he would give him the benefit of the doubt. His keenness to help the War Crimes Unit was highly creditable, but he must not take the law into his own hands. Any threat to the environment, whether from war crimes or otherwise, should be the concern of all.

But he did not think, on balance, that more facilities for monitoring the greenhouse effect in motorway service areas and old folks' artificial ski-run installations were necessarily the answer.

Celebration

German sports officials accused the English Football Association of giving way to political extremists when it announced that England would not play a match in Berlin on April 20, Hitler's birthday, for fear of violence between "neo-Nazi" and "anti-Nazi" hooligans. "We cannot answer the question as to why we weren't told about the significance of the date earlier," said the wondrously named Sir Bert Millichip, president of the Association.

"Probably they" — the Germans — "were as unaware as we were. If people had asked us the birthdays of some of our war leaders, I doubt that we could have told them", Sir Bert explained with all the positively luminous thickheadedness for which high English football administrators have long been admired.

Meanwhile Sir Roland Grampus-Smith, the genial, unpopular chairman of Stretchford United, which dropped through the bottom of the league tables some time ago but is now back again thanks to a grant from Stretchford Arts (Mime Division), will be celebrating Hitler's birthday rather quietly this year. There will be just a few like-minded directors of the club and members of the Chamber of Commerce with their heavily fur-coated women-folk gathered at his £2 million Tudorbethan mansion in leafy, watchtower-guarded Lampton-on-Hoke.

There will be none of the lavish pleasures of former years, when star players such as Albert Rasp, the world-famous goal-conceding goalkeeper, were chained up and forced to entertain the guests after dinner. Sir Roland would amuse them by condemning Rasp to death by various gruesome means, then reprieve him at the last moment. Rasp, who would stare, totally unmoved, into his boots throughout, was tearfully grateful for the coins of low denomination Sir Roland flung him as lie crawled out backwards on all fours.

There was always a ritual demonstration by a force of students from Stretchford University commanded by the veteran sociology student Ken Slabb, perpetual president of the students' representative council. Just as they seemed about to take the place by storm, Sir Roland would order his personal pack of Tibetan mastiffs to be unleashed. And as the demonstrators fled in panic an unquenchable laughter arose.

End of an Error

On the day of Jackie Onassis's funeral, with a perfect sense of occasion, rain fell even more incessantly and pitilessly on Stretchford than on other English cities. In a solemn ceremony of reconciliation, high officials of the Our Jackie Onassis and Anti-Our Jackie Onassis Fan Clubs met in historic Victoria Square outside the Nadirco Hyper-consumerama, scene of so many epic confrontations, to declare both the rival clubs "defunct from this moment of time to eternity".

Tattered battle flags were lowered. Iron-tipped outsize handbags and sawn-off umbrellas — traditional weapons now largely superseded by the more up-to-date bazooka or experimental nuclear device — were carried at the trail or reversed as these formidable women, many of the "ogress-type" believed to be indigenous to this area of the West Midlands, filed round the square in a slow march. The rival anthems were sung for the last time and simultaneously, producing an unusual musical effect, which had many reaching for ear-plug or cough lozenge.

It was, as a special article in the Stretchford Sentinel mentioned more than once, "the end of an era". For the Our Jackie Onassis Fan Club was the very first of all the hundreds of typical housewives' fan clubs devoted at first to the Kennedy family and its connections, later to all kinds of people ranging from Saddam Hussein and Richard Branson to Ayatollah Khomeini, Jacques Delors and Slobodan Milosevic, which have long made life in Stretchford even more unpleasant than it would be otherwise.

The Anti-Our Jackie Onassis Fan Club, most of whose members were middle-aged women who claimed to have been divorced "GI brides" and mistresses of President Kennedy, yet furiously resented his widow's marriage to a Greek shipowner, was remarkable for its extreme ferocity. It is thought that its historic battle in the tinned pet food sector of the Hyperconsumerama with the opposing club, in which the pet food section leader was decapitated and parts of the building set on fire, led to the establishment in 1975 of the Stretchford Police Special Fan Club Squad under its gifted supremo, Supt J.S. Harrogate, now 51, secretary of the local pre-Raphaelite Circle.

Will the disappearance of the two original clubs, asks the Sentinel, "presage the gradual decline of other clubs and perhaps, in a veritable Norn-fated cataclysm, the end of the clubs altogether? Some will be glad of their passing, believing that they have no place in our practical, cost-effective age. Yet many will mourn the end of a uniquely picturesque, albeit destructive feature of our beloved city."

At his Fan Club Squad headquarters, where state-of-the-art electronic wall-maps registered an unprecedented "all quiet" on the fan club front and his normally hyperactive team of picked policewomen sat listlessly about, a stunned Harrogate could only murmur, "The old order changeth, yielding place to new", while the squad cat Blackie, nine, stared balefully at him with yellow eyes through dried sunflowers in a purple vase.

Battlefields

English Heritage's list of battlefields does not include a single one in the Stretchford Conurbation. But this does not worry the Tourism, Leisure and Heritage Department of the Stretchford Metropolitan County Council under its dynamic director, Dr Aylwin Goth-Jones. "Our battlefields," he says, "are second to none in Britain in tourism potential, environmental value and educational and interpretational outreach."

Some of the sites, according to the department's panel of historians, some of whom hold university degrees and have even appeared on television chat shows, are disputed. Some are "composite battlefields" where several battles are believed to have been fought at different times or even at the same time.

The battle of Gnomesall Heath, for example, where the Parliamentarians under Fairfax are said to have defeated a Royalist army under General John Colsterworth in 1643, is also thought to be the site of a battle between Yorkist and Lancastrian forces in 1468, and before that of a skirmish (c 657) between the forces of the wicked King Penda of Mercia and a band of heavily armed monks under "the militant hermit and Robin Hood lookalike" St Oick of Stretchford, in which Penda's pagan warriors took a terrible beating.

The advantage of this wealth of history is that all these battles can be included in the same theme park, one of the projected "flagship" installations of Nadirleisure, the amenity division of the giant Nadirco Consortium. The Stretchford Battlefield Theme Park, due to open next spring, will have an unrivalled collection of "battle informational facilities", a casino, ice rink, disco, old folk's artificial ski-run, marina "for all the family", bowling alleys, sex advice and "family planning" arenas, putting greens, a pick-your-own farm produce area (one of the Seth Roentgen Merrie Olde Englande chain), a four-star hotel with jousting area and business conference centre staffed by teenage models

In the kiddies' adventure playground there will be one of the largest concentrations of inflatable castles and shoot-yourself crossbow facilities in the country.

Calling All Bores

By '*Narcolept*'

It was bound to happen! For months now the question of admitting members of the "gay community" (do you recall those far-off days when it used to be called, more picturesquely, but alas, less boringly, the "mauve international"?) to full parity on the professional boring scene has been argued intensively among the high-ups of the British Board of Boring Control. On the face of it, it's hard to see how they've held out so long.

It's 20 years now since the Board, after long and heated controversy, voted narrowly to admit women bores into the charmed circle of the boring elect. No woman bore has yet made it to the top flight, to claim a place beside such all-time greats as Antonin Bvorak of Czechoslovakia that was, Prem Krishna Nattacharya of India, or Jean-Pierre Cafard of Canada. But we may take it for granted that the fair sex nowadays has bores to boast of equal to all but the very greatest. Soon, the way things are going, female bores (shades of Miss Dworkin, Miss Wolfe, Miss Hite, to name but a few) may even surpass them!

Twenty years ago all this would have been unthinkable! But women bores now regularly take part in the Intergalactics at Harringay, welcomed by all but a few diehards to that Mecca of aficionados of the yawn game the world over. Yet so far, with the mighty drone of that legendary veteran drowse maestro Sir Herbert Trance, the much revered President of the BBBC, still sounding against them, the advocates of equal status for the "gay community" have not prevailed.

Among some of us youngsters, I suppose, it is a common view that "queers", as an exotic minority, have been guilty all too often of the cardinal sin of seeming to be "interesting", which has, of course, ruled them out of our grand old sport on principle. But in view of the present controversy on homosexual rights, which has reached heights of sheer 24-carat tedium greater than any comparable phenomenon in my lifetime, how can these people be reasonably excluded any longer?

A "community" which can produce a stupendous bore like the Great Tatchell, to name but one contemporary homosexual coma merchant of near-genius, must have a wealth of unused talent which might do much to benefit the game. You may not agree, but in my view the BBBC, as it endlessly debates the issue in the fabled halls of London's Tedium House, will sooner or later find it has to come to terms with our modern age.

And by the way, boring fans who think this superbly yawnworthy controversy will fade away once equal boring status is granted can dismiss their fears at once. Believe me, it will go on forever, an unfailing inspiration to us all.

How It Works

"Most historians," says a reviewer in the Guardian, "accept the profound influence African civilisation had on that of ancient Greece." Well, do they? This idea can be traced to the historian Martin Bernal's book Black Athena and its sequel. The influence of ancient Egyptian civilisation on that of Greece has certainly been accepted by historians from Herodotus onwards. How "profound" that influence was is another matter.

Bernal moved the idea into a new, highly fashionable dimension by stressing the profundity of the influence and somehow implying that because the ancient Egyptians lived in Africa they must have been black; therefore it was "black African civilisation" which profoundly influenced that of Greece.

The ancient Egyptians were not black; nor from the evidence of their pictorial remains did they ever suppose they were. But what does that matter, when there are political dividends to be gained? Here is a fine example of a highly dubious academic theory which has got into the popular consciousness and is already turning, by the ineluctable law which governs such matters, from a mere theory into an accepted belief.

Today it is taken as reasonable by reviewers in the *Guardian*. Tomorrow it will be the common belief ("the ancient Greeks were black") of people who know nothing of historical research and care less. A little later it will be compulsory to believe it, and those who don't will be execrated as wicked or mad — and, even worse then either, as "racists" of the most abandoned kind.

A Wonderful Job

A Traffic Warden in Devon claims he was forced to retire early because of excessive zeal. He is said to have followed a bus driver into a public lavatory to give him a parking ticket, booked a motorist who was picking up a prescription for his sick wife and even booked a whole coach full of disabled people.

"I have been penalised for doing my job properly," he says. He is evidently a man who takes pride and pleasure in his work, and it is easy to see why. If the job of traffic warden were better paid, it would be one of the most sought-after jobs of all. It has almost every attraction; it offers a smart uniform which commands, if not respect, a small but significant degree of fear; a life in the open air with plenty of moderate exercise. Above all it has the thrill of the chase and the satisfaction of the kill.

I once overheard a group of women traffic wardens gleefully discussing the day's doings. "Had a real bit of luck this morning." one said. "Slapped a ticket on a brand-new Jag — only 45 on the clock!" Though envious of her triumph, the rest fell about laughing.

What became of the fashion in the Sixties for well-off middle-class traffic wardens who worked for nothing? I believe they were allowed to have their own uniforms made to measure of costly cloth, or silk and brocade with gold or jewelled shoulder-badges. Some carried clouded canes. Perhaps it was this over-gorgeousness which set not only motorists but also humbler traffic wardens against them and drove them off the streets. You certainly don't see them about nowadays.

What the Papers Say

In a thoughtful leader, *The Feudal Times and Reactionary Herald* discusses the row over Harriet Harman's son's education: "... Even when the victim is that almost ultimate absurdity, a woman member of Parliament, we must deplore the intrusion of politics into what should be a purely personal matter. That said, there is something unmistakably ludicrous in the spectacle of both the principal factions in Parliament exchanging insults and accusations of hypocrisy on questions of education.

"Both the so-called 'Conservative' faction and the so-called 'Labour' faction habitually boast of a commitment, often transparently insincere, to the pernicious principle of 'equality' in education. As to which faction is the more guilty of rank hypocrisy we must leave closer students of that all too human failing to decide. The root cause of the present disastrous state of education in England lies in the fatal concept of compulsory, universal education which has, during the last century, gained such a hold on the public mind that, save in our own columns, it is scarcely ever questioned.

"A fallacy, enormous in every sense, underlies the whole concept. For it must be apparent to every unprejudiced mind that a large part of the population neither desires nor needs nor is capable of any formal learning beyond that required for simple reading and writing and elementary arithmetic. To enforce anything more is simple cruelty. It is liable to make such people discontented, envious, incapable of performing the ordinary, necessary tasks of life and, above all, wanting in that proper respect for their betters without which they are unfitted for a humble yet useful place in society.

"Who can wonder that many take to a life of crime? The gradual elimination of this false and mischievous system of education is essential if we are to restore the natural order of things. That the ruling class or that portion of it concerned with government, must be suitably educated goes without saying. On the other hand, there is no reason why gifted, meritorious sons even of labourers — for such undoubtedly exist — should not be encouraged and helped to rise in the world as they have always done.

"The aim must be a nation in which all — master and servant, craftsman and apprentice, yeoman farmer and hireling shepherd — are educated, if at all, according to their needs, abilities and place in society, and not according to a narrow, mechanical system arbitrarily imposed by quacks, theorists and demented projectors."

Pedants' Corner

As a partisan of the Irish language, I am pleased with the growing fashion for spelling Irish surnames in correct Gaelic style: eg, Dr Máire ní Bhrolacháin, the Senior Lecturer in Population Studies at Southampton University, briefly in the news for having had nude paintings removed from the walls of a seminar room.

Having to keep telling people how her name is pronounced may be tiresome for her, but it is a small price to pay. It is a price some other Irish notabilities are evidently not prepared to pay. Mr Martin McGuinness of Sinn Féin, for instance, does not insist on the correct spelling of his surname, Mac Aonghusa, when he is engaged in the "peace process". Nor (a more extreme case) did Mr Haughey, the former Prime Minister, insist on 0 hEochaidh at all times, as I certainly would have done had I been in his place.

De Valera declared he would rather have Ireland Gaelic-speaking than united. He believed, I think rightly, that without her mother tongue Ireland can never be more than half a nation. What would he have thought of such odious examples of spelling-treachery as Aer Lingus (correctly Loingeas) where the base convenience of trade has shamefully prevailed over the fundamental rules of Irish orthography?

Referendum

The recent debate about "Europe", in which various politicians of the different parties made self-contradictory statements, must have left any voters who were paying attention more confused than ever. There was much talk of a referendum on the "single currency". One personage who took particular offence at this was Sir Edward Heath, "the man who took us into Europe".

European experience, he said, had shown how difficult it was to get voters in a referendum to answer the question. That depends on how the question is put. Heath, you may think, should be the last to complain on that score.

In the referendum on "Europe" in the Seventies, as far as I can remember that dismal fraud, voters were not asked to say whether or not they wanted Great Britain to be in "Europe" at all. They were merely asked whether they wanted Great Britain to remain in it. A majority of those who actually voted said yes, perhaps because it is more comfortable to keep things as they are rather than change them.

These deluded people did not know that what they had voted for was in fact changing all the time, and in a direction they did not want: that is, towards a European Federation. It will surely not be difficult to devise an equally misleading question for a referendum on the "single currency", again taking adherence to "Europe" for granted. It is not for me to suggest what it might be. That is for subtler minds than mine.

But a hint, conveyed in suitably obfuscatory language, that if voters do not vote in favour they will lose all or most of their own currency might do the trick.

Anniversary

Veterans of the Royal Army Tailoring Corps, the elite force founded by Lt Gen Sir Frederick ("Tiger") Nidgett which played a key part in the Second World War, are angry at being excluded from the official "VE-Day" celebrations. They had hoped to take part in a victory march through London with their mobile armoured sewing machines and other weapons, which struck terror and amazement into the German army. But it was not to be.

In his volume of memories Up Sticks and Away, the "Tiger" tells the epic story of the Ratcorps' stand at Port Said when "Rommel and his Nazi hordes were battering tastelessly at the gates of Egypt, grunting gutturally the while in true Germanic fashion", and of his own daring plan to fall back "in certain eventualities" on Aden, Socotra, Madagascar and "if need be, on the ultimate hinge of peril", New Zealand.

But after the victory in North Africa the Ratcorps were transferred to the European theatre, leaving only a token force in Port Said. Their exploits in mopping up remaining pockets of resistance in the bazaars brought in vast quantities of cloth, buttons, thread and other essential materials of war which were to be of vital importance in the last stages of the war and after.

Based at the Corps Depot in legendary East Ardsley Junction in the West Riding (where their operations met with much stiffer resistance), the Ratcorps were, as Nidgett complained in many an angry protest to the War Office, "woefully under-stretched". His proposal that the RAF should drop thousands of explosive coat-hangers over Germany was turned down flat by "Bomber" Harris, who evidently had other ideas.

Harris, according to Nidgett, declared that the use of coat-hangers as a weapon was "too horrifying to contemplate" and, since they might easily injure civilians, was in any case contrary to the Geneva Convention on the rules of war. "This namby-pamby attitude," writes Nidgett, "may well have lengthened the war by months, if not minutes." Another secret Ratcorps weapon, three-legged trousers with muliple turn-ups, was also turned down. "All in all, a sorry tale of weakness, irresolution in high places and inter-departmental jealousy."

Debarred from the celebration in London, the veterans are to hold their own celebration this very Sunday on the holy ground at East Ardsley Junction which became derelict when the Corps was disbanded in 1955 (it is now the site of a dog biscuit factory). Today is the 50th anniversary of the presentation of the Trouserpress of honour to Stalin by a delegation of "Left-wing" Ratcorps men headed by Sgt Maj Trousercutter Stan

("Jock") Lazarowicz, now chairman of the Ratcorps Veterans' Association and also of Military Tailors against War, now dormant.

"It was just a wee bit return for the Sword of Stalingrad. Stalin was dead chuffed, ye ken," war hero Lazarowicz, scion of a distinguished Edinburgh family, says in his personal Scots dialect. Sadly, there were rumours that the Trouserpress of Honour was damaged later on during a particularly boisterous evening party in the Kremlin; or, worse still, that it was used after Stalin's death to execute Beria by squashing him flat inside it.

A Fine Breed

Crufts again; and an old injustice still persists. Mrs Morag Ironheart, who breeds Clackmannanshire terriers at her kennels at Brig O'Dread in their epymonous county, has again been told that they are not recognised as a breed by the authorities, and so cannot be officially shown.

Yet Mrs Ironheart herself, a large, tough, tweed-clad lady of the good old kind, testifies by her innumerable scars, by her well gnawed brogues and other signs of devotion to the breed that these "game little chaps", as she calls them, have their own unique and loveable qualities.

They were originally used by Highland landlords' factors to help evict crofters and their families at the time of the Clearances. One "clackie" down the chimney and the crofters, with whatever meagre possessions they could grab hold of in time, were haring away down the road to the nearest emigrant ship and the quickest passage to Nova Scotia.

Mrs Ironheart, who allowing for her much greater size and deeper, more thunderous bark is not unlike her dogs, once suggested that, although small and stunted, they might be useful for some kind of police work. But the police, like their own mild and gentle German Shepherd dogs, took much the same view as the Highland crofters, thankful that unlike them, they had solidly built police stations to take refuge in.

More recently Mrs Ironheart, anxious for her dogs to do some useful work in the world, offered half a dozen surplus ones to some Glasgow football fans, so called "keelies" or "poison dwarfs" who resemble them in size, strength and ferocity. It was just as well they declined her offer. It was a question of which would have prevailed over and perhaps eaten, which.

Bias

It is not really a question of the BBC's bias against the Conservative

Party and Government. Any reasonable person is biased against them; some are biased because there is nothing about them which can be called conservative. The BBC's bias is of a larger order.

Because it believes people can be made to behave better by political reform, the Left — and thereby the Labour Party, whether or not it calls itself socialist — long ago annexed the concept of benevolence for the poor and unfortunate. So arose the idea that all who oppose the Left, particularly those who call themselves conservative, are at best cynical, pessimistic or nostalgic enemies of all change: at worst hard-faced, cruel and selfish exploiters of the oppressed.

The kind of people who work for the BBC and the higher levels of the "media" in general are naturally biased to the Left for this reason. They do not think they are biased; they think they have the opinions and attitudes — whether about education or the "multi-racial society" or the United Nations or "majority rule" in South Africa or any such matter — which all people with the least intelligence or decent feeling have.

They think any apparently intelligent or decent person who does not have these opinions and attitudes is either mad or wicked or perversely pretending to be so. As for the rest, they are simply stupid — the despised "instinctive Tories" continually ridiculed in the "media" whether as "upper-class twits" or lower-class "Alf Garnetts".

The Left — and thereby the Labour Party — has contrived to make it appear that it occupies and will always occupy the moral high ground. It does not see itself as biased; it sees itself as right. We may rage against this powerful, pervasive delusion. How to end it is another matter.

A Lofty View

An interesting discussion is going on just now in the correspondence columns of the *Feudal Times and Recreationary Herald*. It is about the proposal, first made when the so-called "European Parliament" arose from the void like a cut-price Pandemonium in the Seventies, for a European House of Lords which would include representatives of the ancient nobility of all the countries in the so-called "European Union".

You might expect that your average reader of the *FTRH* — if the term is permissible — would regard the idea of a European House of Lords with even more abhorrence than other "European" institutions, finding it as insolent a contradiction in terms as can be imagined. But some of the younger feudal reactionaries think that once a European House of Lords was established, it might, by continually imposing a ponderous and majestic veto, be able to render the whole "European" business inoperable.

Even if it had no statutory powers, one Peer of the Realm writes, "Might not the sheer antiquity of our titles of nobility gradually spread its awesome shadow of authority over the petty activities of the jumped-up clerks, decayed tapsters and mercenary bagmen who now presume to busy themselves with the concerns of that false Europe they have devised in their own base image?

"As these creatures scurry about from committee to committee in Brussels, Strasbourg or Luxembourg, pursuing their petty money-making schemes and spinning their paper webs of ever more superfluous legislation, may they not come to hear an insistent interior voice recalling each one of them, whether his forebears were peasants, moneylenders or sturdy beggars, to a sense of his own humble place in the unchanging hierarchical order of things?"

Few noblemen, to judge from the correspondence in the *FTRH*, take this hopeful view. But many upper servants, it seems, would like to see a European House of Lords, if only for the advantages for themselves in their masters' attendance. One of the most enthusiastic is the Earl of Mountwarlock's factotum Phantomsby, one of the few practising werewolves left in the Midlands and probably the only one to take any interest in European affairs.

Unlike many people, Phantomsby is quite fond of foreign tourists, particularly large well-nourished Germans and appetising Scandinavians, and welcomes them to his master's "stately home" in Leicestershire. But the chances of the Earl taking his seat in a future European House of Lords are small.

For one thing, he has not left Mountwarlock for several hundred years. For another, his family traits — he is over eight feet tall and has a Cyclops eye in the middle of his forehead — might be used as arguments by opponents of the hereditary principle.

Deep Matters

A discussion about Darwinism in the *Independent* addresses a fundamental question: how did the "selfish gene" of Dr Dawkins's well-known bestseller come to allow goodness into the world? The answer, according to the Darwinists, lies in the "rapidly expanding discipline of evolutionary psychology". This shows that although the "selfish gene" is the unit of replication on which the process of natural selection works, it is the degree of social organisation of the host organism and its development of social bonds, which decide the gene's survival. Altruism expresses and reinforces those bonds. Thus came goodness into the world.

In this way, according to one Darwinist, "evolutionary psychology is set to explain all the more attractive aspects of human nature in strictly Darwinian terms... The hardest truth of Darwinism is still to come, but it is coming."

Why this overbearing, almost threatening tone? Why this note of unmistakable triumph over those who go on clinging to old ideas of human goodness as something inexplicably and supernaturally given? Why do these scientists take such obvious pleasure in putting them down? Is this a manifestation of the selfish gene, which will ensure the perpetuation of revolutionary scientists; or, on the other hand, lead by its extreme self-satisfaction to their eventual extinction?

Suppose they are right about goodness in this world, necessarily the only world they believe in. It is a world they share with millions of simple-minded and highly suggestible people quite unlike themselves. Is it right that such a pitiless doctrine of collectivism should be allowed to filter into these people's minds and lives, inevitably in a crude, popularised form, persuading them that they are animals like the rest and that the collective will must be the ultimate reason for everything they do?

For most people the world of the future is going to be rough, crude and violent enough. It is certainly not going to be a world of quiet, well-ordered research laboratories. Is it right for these scientists, mostly reasonable, mild-mannered people with no great love of violence themselves, to risk making it more violent for the mass of people? How do they know, anyhow, that they will be immune themselves? For them too there may be nothing to cling to but the collective.

When the authorities of the Church condemned Galileo for asserting that the earth moved round the sun, they were quite well aware that it did so, as astronomers had been aware in ancient times. But they rightly believed that from a moral point of view it did not matter in the least whether the earth moved round the sun or the sun moved round the earth or each moved round the other.

Their concern was to "save the appearances": to confirm unreflective people in their belief that the earth where they lived was the centre of Creation; and thus to foster a healthy human belief in the primacy of unchanging moral laws over changing "scientific fact" and pointless worries about the precise motions of the heavenly bodies.

The theories of evolutionary psychology touch human lives far more closely than the astronomical theories of Galileo. What would the Inquisition have done to curb evolutionary scientists and control the probable effect of their doctrines, far more dangerous and deadly than those of Galileo for the unreflecting mass of mankind and far more convenient for its future masters? Unfortunately we have no Inquisition now.

Walls Galore

"English Heritage" is a strangely named body whose activities grow
stranger and stranger to correspond. One of its ideas is to "sell off"
hundreds of its craftsmen to private enterprise. This is part of a plan to
contract out the maintenance and repair of such monuments as Stone-
henge, Dover Castle and Hadrian's Wall.

"Heritage" bodies like the Ancient Monuments Society are worried
that restoration work may fall into unskilled hands. "The job of repointing
Hadrian's Wall", says one expert, "cannot be given to a bricklayer used
to a three-bedroomed semi". I am not so sure of that. There are archaeologists who believe that the men who built and maintained Hadrian's
Wall were by no means highly qualified craftsmen by the standards of
modern heritage experts.

Excavations have shown that a stretch of the Wall near Newcastle
had no foundations and that early in the third century the southward face
collapsed and was never repaired. Altogether the Wall seems to have
been incompetently designed and shoddily built. What is more, it was
covered for much of its length with hideous gleaming white plaster, no
doubt satisfactorily terrifying to barbarians but extremely offensive to
any Romano-British persons of taste who may have been about.

Some archaeologists believe that the Wall made no strategic sense
but was hastily run up for profit by "bent" contractors in collusion with
Roman planning officials and wall fanatics, rather in the way more and
more unnecessary roads are built all over the country today. No blame,
of course, attaches to Hadrian himself, an admirable and conscientious
emperor. But even he could not keep an eye on everything all the time,
particularly in remote corners of his Empire.

It is possible that large numbers of these pointless walls were planned
all over Roman Britain. Some may actually have been built, infuriating
people who were moved out of the way by compulsory purchase and
then done out of the meagre compensation offered by contractors who
threatened to "send round some of our barbarian lads to see you for a bit
of a chat", even though there might be no barbarians for hundreds of
miles.

Recent finds of catalogues in tablet form giving detailed quotations
for various types of wall ("run you up a lovely job, quaestor — guaranteed top quality rubble and plaster — everybody's begging for them —
mind you, you'll be looking at the region of, well, say two million sestertia

at the end of the day") show that not everything may have been, as the saying was, entirely on the level.

Honour

After a strikingly devious political career, the dying François Mitterrand, retiring President of France, has seemed honourably anxious to tell the truth before he dies, even at the cost of embarrassment and outrage. For example, in a speech during the VE celebrations he made a point of praising the bravery of wartime German soldiers, courage being courage, as he said, whatever uniform men may be wearing.

This undoubted truth set off automatic screams of ignoble fury. A M. Jacques Attali, who is, I think, a prominent banker or "Euro-financial expert" or something of that sort, and for all I know has never worn a military uniform of any kind, said the only German soldier worthy of respect was a deserter or one who refused to serve a bad cause.

He might, I suppose, have taken his argument to its logical conclusion: that the only Russian soldier worthy of respect was a deserter or one who refused to serve a cause equally bad and even more persistently terrible in its effects.

In fact, hundreds of thousands of Russian soldiers did desert in the last war. Many in their burning desire to overthrow the communists who had enslaved their countrymen served on the German side and were handed over to the murderous care of Stalin after the war was over.

History, which belongs to the victors, has not been kind to these men. No Attali will speak for them. But one day — who knows? — history, if there is any, may make amends.

Goodweel's Rule

"I see that a couple in Yorkshire have chosen to have their marriage blessed at a motorway service station. What do you think of that, padre?" J. Bonington Jagworth, Britain's most eminent motorist, laughingly addressed this question to the Rev John Goodwheel, chaplain-general to the Motorists' Liberation Front, known to millions as the "Apostle of the Motorways".

Goodwheel, who had just got back from a mission to the southwest in his mobile romanesque cathedral, pondered the matter gravely, fingering the gold pectoral spanner which hangs from his neck. "This is undoubtedly a step forward towards the coming synthesis of religion and motoring in a very real sense," he said.

"This couple have realised that there are no places where the sense of the sacred can be felt more deeply and inwardly than in our motorway service stations. For some people, it is true, the roundabout or interchange, which leads to many roads, many choices, many alternatives, with some, of course, leading nowhere, seems to encapsulate the essential mystery of things. But I believe, in all humility, that they are mistaken!"

"Then you think," said Jagworth, "you're going to have a lot of couples asking you to bless them at service stations when they get hitched up? Won't there be trouble with different sects, or Buddhists, Muslims and suchlike? I mean you don't want some motoring ayatollah handing out a nasty fatwa, do you?"

Goodwheel spread oil-stained hands in a pious gesture. "In my view, our service stations are ecumenical or they are nothing. They represent the convergence of all human beliefs. They prefigure the service stations of heaven, where neither rust not moth corrupt and the Boggs Super Yobbo shall be equal with the Lada Popular...." But Jagworth was already snoring.

Speculations

Asked what he thought about the Second World War, the Sinn Fein leader Gerry Adams described it as an "imperialist adventure". These are, of course, the precise terms which British communists, following the official Moscow line, would have used to describe the war from 1939, the year of the Nazi-Soviet pact, until the German invasion of Russia in 1941.

Is this still the official thinking of Sinn Fein? Or is Adams stuck fast in a personal time warp? His pronouncement naturally annoyed many people. What, they asked, would have happened to Ireland if the Germans had won the war?

This is a very interesting question. The Germans would certainly have tried to set up a puppet state in Ireland north and south, perhaps on the lines of Slovakia, though of greater strategic importance for the future wars Hitler was already gloatingly dreaming about.

But whom would they have got to run it? The fanatical anglophobes of the South and the forebears of the current Provisionals? The great Irish Protestant historian Hubert Butler shrewdly surmised that these people might have been in for a nasty shock. He thought the Nazis, on "racial", historical and above all practical grounds, might have preferred a United Irish Republic run by more efficient and reliable people: the hard Protestant men of the North.

But as the maladroit Nazis tried to woo these formidable people to their side wouldn't they very likely have been in for an even nastier shock themselves?

Pioneer

Correspondence between Charlotte Brontë and Robert Southey has come to light. In 1836 Miss Brontë wrote to Southey, then Poet Iaureate, about her "wish to be a poet". He replied in due course, admitting that she had "the faculty of verse" but warning her against committing herself to being a poet. He advised her to shun "the daydreams in which you habitually indulge".

"Literature," he wrote, "cannot be the business of a woman's life, and it ought not to be." Miss Brontë should "write poetry for its own sake" while attending to her "proper duties" as a woman. Miss Brontë, replying to what she rightly called "kind and wise" advice, undertook to follow it, though she added somewhat pertly: "In the evening, I confess, I do think, but I never trouble anyone else with my thoughts," To which Southey sensibly replied: "Take care of over-excitement."

A timely warning. To fashionable opinion at present, of course, Southey seems merely pompous and absurd, while Miss Brontë's respectful reply seems a "brilliant exercise in veiled sarcasm". We should not be too certain that this will always be so. Unlikely as it may seem, a time may come when the old order of things to which Southey and Miss Brontë both subscribed, with a belief in the proper roles of the sexes, may return again. Discuss.

Further light is shed on this correspondence by a passage in Julian Birdbath's seminal work The Quest for Doreen Brontë, or rather it would be shed if this profound work of scholarship were not so far out of print as to be virtually invisible. Doreen, the so-called "Missing Brontë Sister" discovered by Birdbath in one of the greatest feats of literary detection in history, seems to have intervened in the exchanges between Miss Brontë and Southey in a way completely typical of her.

A strongly-built, pipe-smoking, open-air, no-nonsense kind of woman with an interest in small-bore rifle shooting and electrical engineering and no interest in poetry whatsoever, Doreen had no more patience with her sister's daydreams than she had with her own "proper duties" as a woman. Indeed, when, without asking Charlotte's permission, she snatched Southey's letter and read it, she gave a stupendous guffaw which

made the Parsonage's windows rattle and had Branwell running in panic
to the shelter of the snug in the Black Bull at Haworth. "She's broken out
again," he told his cronies. "Aye, 'appen," they said cautiously. "It certainly makes you pensive."

Meanwhile Doreen, who had a half-contemptuous affection for her
weakling sisters, offered to go and "duff Southey up" or "do him over",
whichever Charlotte preferred. She would have done both if Charlotte,
who had her literary career to think of, had not begged her to stay her
hand.

So this early feminist pioneer was done out of a chance of striking a
blow for the Women's Movement and teaching the predecessor of Ted
Hughes a lesson he would never have forgotten. Did Doreen, Birdbath
speculates, dimly foresee the feminist literary feuds of today and bitterly
regret that she was born too soon to muscle in on them?

Will justice ever be done? Will the achievement of Birdbath, who
now lives in a disused lead mine in Derbyshire with only his pet toad
Amiel for company be recognised at last, his books republished, his due
place in English letters acknowledged? Will there be a Doreen Brontë
Chair of Women's Studies at Keighley University? That, as the saying
is, will be the day.

Digging Away

Amateur archaeologists, who once worked on "digs" for nothing, complain that they are being squeezed out by professionals. The reason is the
increased government funding of archaeology and a hugely growing
number of students taking courses in archaeology at a hugely growing
number of universities.

One reason for that, of course, is that archaeology is a rather easy
and attractive subject to get a degree in. It can offer a pleasant life in the
open, with plenty of opportunities to make friends and influence people
of the opposite sex on the "dig", and even a chance to appear on television. No wonder professional archaeologists do not want to share their
privileged life with amateurs.

It is all very sad. We have already seen the last of the old style
gentleman antiquarians, one of the glories of England in days when eccentric landowners and clergymen of means used to unearth dubious
Romano-British or "Celto-Iberian" remains in park or meadow. With
these they would beautify their houses or fill up local museums, and
write learned papers, often unsound, in local antiquarian journals about
them.

The present breed of highly organised, commercially aware professionals must regard such people and their papers with patronising contempt, a subject, perhaps, for loud and even coarse guffaws. But what honourable Roman Briton or "Celto-Iberian" — even a phantom one — would not rather have his potsherds dug up by a romantically minded, old-fashioned gentleman than by a brash, soullessly efficient, up-to-date expert from Nerdley University?

Ever Onward

One of the great scandals of our time, now belatedly revealed, is the great "health education" campaign on Aids, which has been got up by various official and semi-official "health" and "safety" organisations backed by the Government. By exaggerating the risk from the disease for the mass of people, they have so far contrived to spend £150 million and debauch the public mind with propaganda of staggering vulgarity and amorality.

Is a reaction setting in? After strong protests, the British Safety Council has had to withdraw a poster it must have been particularly proud of: it showed a picture of the Pope with a slogan: "Eleventh Commandment; Thou shalt always wear a condom".

This may be only an apparent setback. Dr Llewelyn Goth-Jones, the director of community medicine for Stretchtord, thinks that although any publicity for condoms must be good in itself, it may be "counterproductive" to show the Pope in such a serious context.

"Many people may have heard vaguely of the Pope as a notorious relic of medieval superstition. This apparent endorsement by him may put them off wearing condoms, if only for a few minutes, with effects on their physical and mental health we hardly dare contemplate."

Dr Goth Jones is an acknowledged expert on what he and his fellow workers for modern ideals and a better, healthier life for everybody call "our condom culture". As well as being director of community medicine, he runs a chain of "family planning", abortion and "sex education" centres in the West Midlands and hosts the popular GPI Television "phone-in" sex advice programme. "Calling Dr Llew."

He is also a director of Malebolge Pharmaceuticals, an important British subsidiary of the giant consortium Nadirco International.

Arts News

There are yells of anger from the "arts community" at some rather inadequate cuts in grants to the Arts Council and thousands of other bodies engaged in "bringing the Arts to the People" and, where parasitical jobs are concerned, vice versa. In proportion to size, few have yelled louder than Marylou Ogreburg's Multiracial Bread and Marmite People's Street Dance Theatre, now touring the Stretchford Conurbation.

Marylou, a tall, bony woman with lenseless glasses and an unforgettable laugh, comes from Dessentville, Ohio. She claims to have been sentenced to be burned at the stake by Senator McCarthy, then rescued at the last moment by Lillian Hellman. At a hastily summoned press conference, she said: "The Tory Government's typically philistine attitude to the arts is making Britain the laughing stock of the world."

"The grant of a mere £300,000 from lottery funds to Marylou's street theatre has made Britain a pariah among the nations," said Czech-born Vaclav Bvorak, brother of Antonin Bvorak, the world boring megastar. Vaclav's own mime performances have added a new element of chilling horror to Marylou's work and helped her to clear whole streets of their inhabitants.

"I want to shake you Brits out of your buttoned-up, inhibited, emotionally illiterate mindset and make you love and care for everybody like your Princess Diana says," Marylou said, waving her outsize World Aids Day ribbon about for emphasis.

Hugh Disk, the GPI Television Network's chief dance critic, said her new show, We Want an Extra Five Million Pounds from Lottery Funds or We Will Go on Like This Indefinitely, was "a stunning masterpiece of street theatre at its finest, an uncompromising, blazingly compassionate, in-yer-face statement of democratic awareness."

Scottish Affairs

A new American film about Sir William Wallace and the fight for Scottish independence has been annexed for propaganda purposes by the Scottish National Party. "Wallace," says Paul Scott, the party's vice-president, "saw independence as a prerequisite for the common good. He realised that without it the freedom of the country to trade, to develop resources and freely to decide on alliances and its own priorities would be destroyed. In modern times, we have no economic future unless we invest our own resources in that future."

Bold Alex Salmond, the leader of the SNP, emits a more resounding battle-cry:

"William Wallace was a campaigner for Scottish independence. I would have been at his side at the Battle of Stirling Bridge." But would

Wallace have been pleased to find either of these party functionaries at
his side, perhaps getting in the way of his gory fight for freedom with
their incessant jabbering about Scotland's economic future, its priorities, the development of its resources and its role in a medieval European alliance which Wallace, for all his vision of economic growth, might
not have seen clearly as the forerunner of the European Economic Community?

The history of Scotland is no simple matter. It may be news to the
leaders of the SNP that Wallace like almost all the leaders of the wars
for Scottish independence, was of English or Anglo-Norman origin, as
were their enemies. So were and are most of the inhabitants of south-
eastern Scotland, which has always been the main or leading part of the
historic Kingdom of Scotland.

The Lowland Scots are really a superior kind of English, having their
roots in the northern part of the English Kingdom of Northumbria which
was never subdued by William the Conqueror. There is a case for regarding Scotland as "Northumbria Irredenta" and therefore part of England (and, of course, vice versa). To describe Scotland as a "Celtic"
country, as people often do, is simply historical ignorance.

What on earth has all this got to do with the people who run the
American film industry? Not much. In their constant wish to mock and
insult the English by any means available, they must have suddenly realised, to their amazement, that there was a country called Scotland, and
that it would be a nice change from making films about English villainy
in Ireland to make a film about English villainy in Scotland instead.

Will desperate Hollywood producers eventually get round to making
films about English villainy in Wales (Llewelyn the Last, The Guns of
Tonypandy, The Song of Jan Morris)? Or would their historical-finan-
cial advisers warn them in time that there probably wouldn't be much
money in it?

Green Thoughts

"The industrial revolution and its consequences have been a disaster for
the human race." This is the theme of a 35,000-word tract by the man
called "Unabomber"', who in the last 20 years is said to have killed three
people and injured 23 in mail-bomb attacks in America. The tract appeared in full in a special supplement of the Washington Post after
"Unabomber" undertook not to carry out further mail-bomb attacks if it
was published.

It is a complete Luddite Manifesto. It calls for the total overthrow of the industrial system and an end to all technological progress. As far as I can see, there is practically nothing in it which I have not been advocating in this column, on and off, for the last 40 years, though I think in a rather less turgid and repetitive style.

I have been able to do this, strangely enough, without killing or threatening to kill anyone if my observations were not published. But then I am not an American, as "Unabomber" presumably is. In any case, as an orthodox Luddite, I cannot assemble the explosive devices he uses to press his case.

What would happen after a successful revolution against technology such as both "Unabomber" and myself so fervently desire? There we seem to differ. In that beautiful green world beyond the great massacres and explosions, he wants an anarchist utopia where nobody has power over anybody else, a worldwide order like William Morris's vision of the future in News from Nowhere. But I want a world of changeless hierarchy "where a dutiful, contented peasantry tills the soil on the lands of the great abbots and nobles who themselves bear on their broad shoulders the dreaming loads of Church, and State".

There is another difference. "Unabomber", in his barbarous way, presumably wants to exterminate all scientists and technologists. I, more humane, would allow a few who care greatly for such things to continue their weird activities under strict supervision. Partly, this would be to allow for that ineradicable strain of curiosity and perverse ingenuity which belongs to our human nature; partly as a warning to the common people of the horrors they had escaped.

So, for one day in the year a few licensed scientists and technologists would enjoy a limited freedom. For 24 hours they could carry on the experiments they find so fascinating; work in their laboratories; operate their ingenious gadgets, their power stations and motor-cars; even fly their aerial machines in the otherwise unpolluted sky.

But they would know, when midnight tolled from the great cathedral bells, that it was time to put away their dangerous, childish toys for another year and humbly submit themselves to the common good.

Dissent

After 20 years the Americans are trying once again to subdue a peasant people with the ruthless methods of advanced technological warfare. Of course the case is altered. The war in Vietnam was, at least ostensibly, a war against communism in the name of freedom. Now we have a war against nationalism in the name of the "international community", precursor, perhaps, of some future multi-racial, multicultural, all-American World order. And this time we are involved in that war ourselves, eagerly offering our own little contribution to the mighty war machine.

Cruise missiles are hurled from warships in the Adriatic against the Bosnian Serbs, not so much to expel them from the territories they previously conquered — ruthlessly enough — as to strike at the heart of their own homeland. Cruise missiles! There was a time when abhorrence of these weapons was a cardinal principle of the Left. "No to Cruise!" "Cruise Out." and other variants were sprayed on a thousand walls.

This was the cause for which the Women of Greenham Common set up their camps with all their fabled "gates" and "benders" for this they danced and sang and wove their many-coloured balls of wool and flung the impacted, paint-enriched dregs of their stinking cookng-pots at passing Americans.

Now not a single shout is raised in Grosvenor Square. Where once thousands demonstrated with ritual chants against the American Embassy not a single demonstrator can be seen. And even if the Americans, baffled and enraged beyond endurance by the Serbs' defiance, should use even more sophisticated weapons — defoliants perhaps — to smoke these obstinate peasants out of their mountain forests, would anybody in the West raise a murmur of protest?

Is This Your Problem?

By Clare Howitzer

Dear Clare Howitzer — I am 23, just under 5ft tall, weight about 15 stone, with dark hair going a bit sparse on top and am considered quite attractive. I've been reading about the Princess of Wales and how a therapist called Suzette Almanack, I think, has helped her to overcome emotional illiteracy, the curse of us inhibited English people, and be able to talk freely about her troubles.

I work in a office doing a filing job and can't afford a therapist, but I've been putting this good advice into practice by talking about my troubles all the time and trying to get the rest of the staff, who are typically inhibited, emotionally illiterate people, to talk all the time about their troubles as well.

So far, total failure! They just carry on in their emotionally illiterate way and even turn their backs on me. Yesterday the manager, who seems to be exceptionally illiterate emotionally, got so angry with me talking about my troubles that he began shouting and jumping up and down and saying that I was his real trouble, and even threatened to stop me talking by shutting my mouth with sticky tape.

How can I help him to become emotionally literate? (Jill Grobes, Nerdley)

Clare Howitzer replies: You could try sitting on a chair while you do your filing, and stare appealingly at this man with your head on one side as you tell him about your troubles. Then if he doesn't start talking about *his* troubles you could try taping *his* mouth with sticky tape so that he can't. He will then *experience real emotional illiteracy*. It will need patience, Jill, but he may eventually get the point.

If not, write to me again and I will give you the address of a women's karate and kick-boxing club which deals with the problem of emotional illiteracy by new, pioneering methods.

Celebrations

The year 1996, whatever other causes for celebration it may bring, will be a great year for centenaries in the Stretchford Conurbation. A well-funded working party has been set up by the Council's 2,000-strong Leisure, Amenity and Heritage Department to make sure they are celebrated in a fitting manner. Here are a few of the most noteworthy:

Jan 28: Ebenezer Holehead, Founder of the Holehead Brass Teapot Foundry at Gnomesall Heath, and ancestor of Cllr Ted Holehead, leader of the Tories on the present council, b1796.

Feb 7: Opening of the 3rd Class Refreshment Room on No2 Platform, Soup Hales (Dredge Road) LMS Station, 1896; destroyed next day in rioting by temporary alliance of militant temperance workers and disaffected platelayers.

April 2: Sydney Frabb, reputed grandfather of Ron Frabb, teenage world idol, and his sister the former Giselle de Frabazon (now reverted to Joan Frabb), model, TV "agony aunt" and pornographic novelist, b Bog Lane, Stretchford, 1896.

June 15: Official opening of lovely, sex-maniac-haunted Sadcake Park (formerly Old Sadcake Fields) by the then Lord Mayor, Sir James Letch, 1896.

Aug 29: Nerdley-born policeman and amateur astronomer J. B. Mackenzie claims discovery of satellite of Mercury, 1896.

Aug 30: Mackenzie's discovery confuted by Astronomer Royal: commits suicide by jumping from roof of canteen at Stretchford Central Police Station.

Oct 17: *Noctes Stretchfordianae*, essays on local bores by the Rev R. S. Canister, first published 1696.
Nov 8: Ettore Gastropodi, first president of Nerdley Friends of Garibaldi Circle and kinsman of Sir Jim Gastropodi, conductor of Stretchford Municipal Symphony Orchestra, b Poggibonsi, Italy, 1796.
Dec 16: Arrival of Aztec colonists in Stretchford neighbourhood after crossing Atlantic in stone boats, 596.
Dec 31: Last day of year 1896.

Goodwheel's Way

There were strange happenings at Coventry Cathedral when the Provost held a service to mark the centenary of the British Motor Industry. An 1897 Coventry Daimler was driven slowly down the aisle while a brass band played. Outside there were demonstrations by members of Roadpeace, an interesting new development in the protestological field which claims to represent the families of all those who have been killed or injured in motor accidents.

During the litany, which asked forgiveness of God for "environmental pollution from exhaust fumes and the relentless encroachment of new roads into the countryside.... The greed which lays waste the earth", a woman shouted "This is a disgrace — you should be ashamed of yourselves", and walked out. But it is not clear from the report whether she was an "eco-warrior" protesting against cars or a member of J. Bonington Jagworth's Motorists' Liberation Front protesting against this spineless clerical apology for their liberating effects.

There was no doubt about another frenzied woman demonstrator who ran out in front of the congregation and stripped, to reveal her naked body covered with slogans reading "17 Million Dead — Forgive Us", "Reforest the Earth", "The Goddess is Mother of the Nation", and so forth.

While all this was going on, where, many are asking, was the Rev John Goodwheel, chaplain-general to the MLF, known to millions as "the Apostle of the Motorways"? His original plan, to preach a sermon glorifying motoring and denouncing the infidel protesters, seems to have been vetoed by the authorities at Coventry as "provocative". Disgusted, he decided to drive, with his organist-mechanic Mr Diapason Smith on board, to Newbury instead.

There he meant to deliver a tremendous rebuke and call for repentance to some of the businessmen who are said to have spoken treacherously in favour of the "tree people" resisting the building of the bypass. But everything went wrong. Even Goodwheel was forced by fog on the motorway to slow down to a mere 90mph. He was stopped by police, who not only gave him a severe warning but — utmost humiliation — breathalysed him for traces of communion wine, of course with negative results.

Approaching Newbury he lost his way in the fog and found himself involved with security guards of the bypass Construction Company, who threatened to shift his cathedral off the site with earthmoving machinery. Only when his resourceful organist vaulted into the organ-loft and began to play a thunderous toccata, with all stops out, by Rimmer (arr. Saint-Saëns) did the deafened and terrified guards retire.

Nature Diary

By *'Redshank'*

Our part of the countryside, though often said to "make its own weather", has lately been sharing the persistent January fog with other less favoured regions. I peer from my study window into a grey vacancy in which indeterminate shapes seem to move about: a shy dotterel, perhaps, most irresolute of birds, dragging an outsize branch for a nest it will never build; Old Fred the Poacher muffled in his multi-pocketed army surplus greatcoat with a dozen brace of pheasant stowed about his person; a strayed businessman vainly searching for the old afternoon striptease club, long ruined and overgrown with bramble and ivy, buried somewhere in the woods yonder?

Who can say? Perhaps these are merely the phantoms to which the imaginations of us nature diarists are only too prone. What is certain is that the fog in my study seems to be growing even denser than the fog outside, so that I have to grope about even to find my typewriter. That furtive rustling in the corner — can it be Old Brock the badger, whose fondness for antiquarian books is proverbial, trying to make off with the only volume of Stugg's *Lives of the Naturalists* he has not removed already?

I go to investigate and tumble headlong into a telltale heap of beech leaves and old tram tickets amassed, if I am not mistaken, by some creature of the wild to furbish nest or sett and hastily abandoned. Clutching the corner of a filing cabinet slippery with lichen, I stagger to my feet, while your badger's characteristic mocking "Hegh, hegh!" shows that the culprit has already made his escape via drainpipe or kitchen hatch, no doubt helping himself en route to a few of my housekeeper Mrs Aggett's freshly baked jam tarts.

I am reminded of the old rhyme, still to be heard in gunroom and four-ale bar:

When mist and fog do wreathe the plain 'Tis time to mend thy wits again.

Such country sayings, I am certain, often contain a profound ancestral wisdom beyond the grasp of your average cocksure, shallow urban intellectual.

Tit for Tat

We genuine scientists are delighted when modish, publicity-conscious scientists searching for "intelligent life" in other parts of the universe (of course there isn't any) make themselves look ridiculous. For four months an astronomer in Australia picked up an inexplicable signal on his radio telescope at the same time each night. He believed he was listening to a message from "intelligent alien life forms".

But the signals turned out to be from frozen dinners cooking in a microwave in the basement. The staff was asked not to use the oven while the telescope was working. But this will not necessarily end the scientists' troubles. As above, so below. "Intelligent life" apart, signals from a distant star may affect their ovens and turn their dinners to a cinder. And how do they know that undetected signals from their ovens may not travel through space to explode a distant star?

Alternative

"Britain Turns Against the Royal Family" announces the *Independent on Sunday,* at the same time announcing, whether or not in consequence, that it means to be a republican newspaper and find out how a British Republic might work. So much the worse for it; and so much the worse for our poor, collapsing country. All the boring old arguments are here: the alleged absurdity of the hereditary principle; the bad or foolish behaviour of the present royal family; the need to abolish pomp and ceremony, superfluous luxuries "we" can't afford. No doubt many who argue like this are pleased with what they think is their own daring freedom of thought.

But hearing much the same old stuff when it was voiced, though less confidently, 30 or even 40 years ago, I used to I wonder what sort of institutions might replace our own royal customs and ceremonies under a presidency, since no state can do without ceremonies altogether, I had a dismal vision: some dreary old radical politician is taking the presidential salute at a parade in Whitehall, as the People's tanks and drab-uniformed units of the People's Police go rumbling and tramping past, and a smug, sullen or cowed selection of the People looks on and cheers to order.

Today this vision of a British presidential state gives way to something quite different — not worse, but even more contemptible. Some modishly popular figure, some much-applauded big businessman or showbiz eminence, some Branson or Grade, perhaps, is president, and there is no parade to salute. There is only the ultimate expression of a degenerate people's soul: a million-strong rock festival and "one world" rally in an enormous, garish, pandemoniac People's Stadium.

Time of Troubles

Are the columnar intelligence services, once noted for their quiet efficiency, no longer what they were? Why, many are asking, was there no warning whatever of the crisis which suddenly erupted a week ago? Heads, as the saying is, may roll.

The solid block of territory on our western border is customarily occupied by various, usually friendly powers. Last Sunday, suddenly and without warning, it was overrun in overwhelming strength by the forces of the Grand Europhile, Sir Edward Heath, deploying, it was estimated, up to 20 divisions of armoured "European" verbiage with artillery and supporting arms, as well as a terror weapon new to our military experts: a huge photograph of the central part of his own face.

The main threat was obviously to the north, the domain of Booker, a friendly and once allied power. This alone would have been enough to alert our defences. And should Booker be overrun, what then? Might not the invading hordes, drunk with victory, turn upon the column itself, striking through the not easily defended fertile plains of the west to menace the capital?

Once the gravity of the situation was realised, the columnar authorities acted, though tardily, decisively enough. General mobilisation was ordered. In the capital, the great bells of the Basilica tolled without ceasing, answered by the bells of all the towns and villages throughout our territory. The levies of the great nobles stood to arms. Men of the yeomanry and militia reported for duty. Volunteers armed with ancient matchlocks, crossbows, scythes and billhooks began pouring in.

Tribal levies, the wild nomad horsemen who formerly roamed the stony wastes of the then undemarcated northern frontier, galloped about in their excitable way, firing home made guns made from lengths of gaspipe into the air. By contrast, elite troops of the Prince Archbishop's Bodyguard paraded briefly in Sibthorp Square in their splendid uniforms, before leaving for the western border.

In the countryside there was momentary panic. For peasant women, Heath, or "Horrendous Ted" as he is sometimes called, has long been a bogeyman relied on for bringing fractious children to order. Rumours of his approach, with the circulation of his photograph by well meaning but ill advised village elders, led to the traditional exodus. Soon the more timid and suggestible peasants took to the roads with their livestock, wheeling handcarts loaded with their pitiful possessions: wine jars, string beds, grandfather clocks, broken rocking chairs, pot stills, stringless lutes and harps, barometers of antique pattern.

This could be readily dealt with. More serious was an infringement of Article Three of the Columnar Constitution, the Principle of Separate Entitites, which defines the coexistent yet disjunct metaphorical, verbal and topographical planes of the column. Unauthorised elements tried to intervene.

Gen Sir Frederick ("Tiger") Nidgett, in a message from Tailoringdene, his Godalming home, offered to recall veterans of his Royal Army Tailoring Corps to the colours. J. Bonington Jagworth promised a motorised brigade drawn from his Motorists' Liberation Front. Dr. Heinz Kiosk offered counselling and a course in peace studies for all parties to the conflict.

A message from Phantomsby, Lord Mountwarlock's gifted factotum, one of the last practising werewolves in the Midlands, arrived, offering a home for Heath in the "safari park", with Fabulous Monster status. Alternatively, Phantomsby wrote, the elder statesman would be welcome as an honoured guest in his own tenebrous but comfortable quarters till the time of the full moon.

Fortunately Mr R. D. Viswaswami, the sadhu and ayurvedic dentist of lovely, sex-maniac-haunted Sadcake Park, suddenly materialised, dispersed the rebellious entities and then obligingly dispersed himself.

So all day along the noise of battle rolled, as yet beyond our frontiers. But the battle is not over. Slight but persistent seismic shocks, hitherto unknown in our temperate lands, are felt, though so far with no damage more serious than the fall of a precious vase in some nobleman's gallery or a widening crack in some cyclopean architrave.

The supreme Columnar Council has issued its traditional

pronunciamiento: "In this grave emergency, the integrity of our columnar homeland must be our first concern. But we cannot emphasise too
strongly that in the event of any serious threat to the paginal balance of
power this column could not and would not stand idly by." Is this, for
once, quite good enough? Time will tell.

A Nasty Fright

The fate of a tastefully oak-panelled Chinese spy satellite which went
out of control is in dispute. The Russians say it crashed into the North-
east Pacific. The Americans say it crashed into the South Atlantic. No
doubt both have their reasons.

What seems agreed is that the satellite was carrying a mould, made
of pure gold, for printing American banknotes and a diamond button
commemorating Mao Tse-tung's 100th birthday.

Whatever you make of the mould, the diamond button offers a portentous, if somewhat far-fetched bit of symbolism. As everybody knows,
the Chinese mandarinate, under the Celestial Empire, had nine grades
distinguished by buttons of different metals or semi-precious stones worn
in the hat. Mandarins of the first grade, for example, wore a button
made of a transparent red stone, of the ninth grade a button of silver.

Does the Communists' diamond button, which transcends the old
imperial grades, signify the power of China itself embodied in the Emperor Mao, a power both immeasurably old and terrifyingly new? We in
the soft, liberal West, who have foolishly given up our own empires,
believe there will never be any more empires in the world. The Chinese
may have other ideas.

The tyrannical power which conquered Tibet and turned its holy places
into missile firing ranges will not be satisfied with taking Hong Kong
and Macao, or even Taiwan. How do we know it will not reassume the
Mandate of Heaven and try to restore the Middle Kingdom, which in
principle held sway over the whole world, claiming tribute from all its
petty barbarian rulers?

The masters of China have not changed because they wear dull western business suits and uniforms instead of gorgeous robes, and no longer
assess all human knowledge according to the examination system of the
mandarinate. Their neighbours in Mongolia and Korea, in Vietnam and
Indonesia and the Philippines, even in Australia and New Zealand —
and that is only a start — may yet be commanded to tremble and obey.

Crisis

Sotheby's auction catalogue of the late Jacqueline Kennedy Onassis's possessions runs to 580 pages and lists a great variety of objects ("she never sold or gave anything away"), from cheap jewellery to antique furniture and a set of J. F. Kennedy's golf clubs.

The auction has not gone unnoticed in Stretchford, where any mention of Jackie Onassis raises immediate fears of a revival of the historic feud between the Our Jackie Onassis Fan Club and its deadly enemy, the Anti-Our Jackie Onassis, as well as equally dangerous outfits like the Revisionist Anti-Our Jackie, the Environmental Our Jackie and innumerable others.

The two original Jackie clubs were, of course, the first of the typical housewives's fan clubs which have done so much to make life in the Stretchford Conurbation even more disagreeable than it would be otherwise. On Jackie's death, the principal clubs devoted to her closed down by mutual agreement. Now people are asking: will the bad old days return?

Mrs Lynne Globes, former president of the Our Jackie, who has a copy of Sotheby's catalogue, said yesterday: "There are a lot of questions we want answering (*sic*). Over the years we sent a great many presents to Our Jackie in token of our esteem. In the fullness of our hearts we did not stint useful offerings like cakestands, knitting patterns and pressure-cookers surplus to our own requirements. I believe the Anti-Our Jackie scum also sent presents such as stale rock buns, defective electric toasters, pokerwork mats with insulting mottoes, joke rubber boa-constrictors and so on.

"But what we all want to know is this: what has become of those presents? They aren't in the catalogue. If Our Jackie kept everything, where is the cerise and Nile-green cardie I sent her in April 1979? If these things are hidden among Our Jackie's relics, we are entitled to have them back, free or for nominal sums, and no messing about, or else."

In a thoughtful leader, the *Stretchford Evening Sentinel* comments: "A single wrong move may trigger an explosion of mindless violence whose consequences no one can foresee. Some may regret the demise of these fan clubs, an element of the picturesque in our often humdrum environment. But the more level-headed will agree that such acts as attacking check-out points in supermarkets with home-made flame-throwers have no place in a democratic, multicultural consumer society".

Alone

A school at Potgietersrus, in the Northern Province of South Africa, which had enforced a whites-only rule for more than 100 years, has been forced to accept a court ruling that it must take black pupils. While the white parents threatened and grumbled, and some kept their children from the school, a black parent, triumphantly heralding the new dispensation, proclaimed: "This is history!"

Liberal thinkers in this country are overjoyed. Not since the hapless attempt to invade Bophuthatswana three years ago, when members of a Boer "commando" were filmed being shot dead by a black policeman as they tried to surrender, has there been such gloating, not only in Mrs Dutt-Pauker's circle but in circles far humbler.

One journalist, in a mean-minded article cleverly entitled "Last of the Laager Louts", mocks those respectable, not perhaps very bright Boer parents for their attempt to "play the culture card", their claim to be protecting their traditions, their "Christian values and mother tongue". Isn't the Boer culture, narrow and dreadfully unfashionable as it may be, as well worth defending as our own relentlessly expanding mass culture of fatuous hedonism?

It seems to me that any person of decent feeling, capable of questioning the conventional opinions enjoined on us, must have some sympathy for these beleaguered people, most execrated of all the world's minorities. Suddenly, after years of being reviled and threatened, they find their world turned upside down. Theirs was an unjust society. But what society ever made by human beings was not?

These jeers and insults come badly from complacent English people who have not known — yet — what it is like to be trapped in a desperate historical impasse. Why should the Boers be blamed for not instantly conforming to fashionable views of absolute human equality, dubious in principle and likely to be disastrous in practice? Why should it be thought right for people to force themselves, where they are not wanted?

Hopeless and lost the Boer cause may be. But for trying to defend it, to defy the world's abuse and mockery and remain themselves, the Boers deserve to be admired rather than condemned.

Cosmic Racism

As well as babbling in their low-minded way about "peanut-shaped bulges and bars" in the galaxies, and what they call, with unearthly vulgarity, the "Snickers hypothesis", astronomers believe they have discovered several "brown dwarfs" within 150 light-years of the Sun. They think these may be plentiful throughout the universe, accounting for the "dark matter" which has caused astronomers so much puzzlement and worry.

This accords with the views of Dr E. J. Multimer of Stretchford University, the first of the so-called "angry young astronomers" who emerged in the Fifties to denounce cosmic awe, thumb their noses at the Universe, and jeer at "the eternal silence of infinite spaces lark". They aimed to assert the equality of all celestial bodies, whether stars, planets, asteroids or comets, and establish a truly classless and democratic universe.

Dr Multimer has now taken his campaign further. "There is no doubt," he says, "that brown dwarfs are grossly discriminated against in favour of other bodies, sneered at by astronomers for their unattractive appearance, and generally denied their cosmic rights. There is an ugly element of institutionalised racism here. I am determined to do all I can to stamp it out.

"It is time the Commission for Racial Equality extended its activities, which have been earthbound far too long, throughout the universe.

"Now that brown dwarfs, so long a persecuted and exploited minority, prove to be numerous and essential to the cosmic community, they should be helped to achieve their proper status, if necessary by measures of positive discrimination.

"I want to see puffed up stars like Betelgeuse and Arcturus and all that toffee-nosed lot, with their oh-so-superior stellar magnitudes and other unearned privileges, cut down to size. We have got to get rid of obsolete deferential attitudes if we are to build a classless, socially just universe of fair shares for all."

A Bishop's Home

The new Bishop of Peterborough, Dr Ian Cundy, has decided to live with his family in his episcopal palace, unlike his predecessor, Dr Westwood, who declared: "I cannot ask other people to make economies ... if I fan around this great big place." Dr Cundy, happily, does not use such ignoble language. But there is an unfortunate note of apology in what he says about his palace. "We hope we can turn it ... into a place where the people and clergy of the diocese will feel welcome and ... a base for the healthy variety of interests and hobbies of a normal family."

What is missing from these well-meaning remarks is any sense of the bishop's palace as a place of awe and majesty, a visible assertion of that episcopal authority which alone can rescue the Church of England from

its present ignominious state. How are the people and clergy to look up
to a bishop who not only seems normal himself but has a normal family?

At least Dr Spacely-Trellis, the go-ahead Bishop of Bevindon, would
never make such a claim. Although he and his "partner", the militant
feminist and former deaconess Mantissa Shout, now Dean, failed, amid
a certain amount of ridicule, to get themselves accepted as members of
the "gay community", they have proved their anti-family, anti-patriar-
chal, multicultural and generally progressive credentials in other ways.

The Bishop gave up his palace years ago (it has become a "family
planning" clinic), and now lives at the "Bishop's Squat" in Ecumenical
Road. It is a conversion of a group of old workmen's cottages, with a
large garden nearby on the site of former allotments from which the
occupants were expelled by a special environmental planning order.

It is somewhat larger than the old bishop's palace. As well as the
Bishop's own quarters, with offices, library and computer centre, and
Mantissa's separate wing, it has a conference hall, pop music rooms,
indoor swimming pool, fully equipped gymnasium, sex education cinema, a mosque, a Hindu temple and "all-faith facilities".

"As a diocesan centre for a forward-looking Church adapted to the
needs of the average man and woman in our secular society," says the
Bishop, "it is free of those vestiges of medieval superstition which still
linger in other dioceses, particularly in the shape of unnecessarily large,
ostentatious palaces. It is a bishop's home for today and tomorrow in a
very real sense."

Foiled Again

In their plans to modernise the armed forces, successive governments
have long had their eye on that bastion of custom and privilege, the
Royal Stretchfordshire Yeomanry, described by the present Adjutant,
Captain the Hon. H. D. T. F. X. Haggard-Jelkes, in his regimental history, as "a veritable inferno of tradition, a long-drawn-out bugle-blast
neighing through the tattered banners of an heroic past".

No wonder malignant governments of levellers and foaming radicals
have tried to humiliate this historic regiment by amalgamating it with
such units as 25 Field Bakery or the defunct Holding Unit (Lapels) of
General Nidgett's Royal Army Tailoring Corps, based at East Ardsley
Junction in the West Riding.

Thanks to the obduracy and cold disdain of the present Commanding
Officer, Col J. S. D. St J. de Z Lestrange-Haggard TD, all these attempts
have failed. But not long ago, in a particularly cunning plan to destroy

the regiment from within, one of the first "race relations" monitors, whose duty it is to enforce "anti-racism" in the Army, was attached to the officers mess at Regimental H.Q. at Lampton-on-Hoke.

The general rule in the mess is that the port is passed clockwise or anti-clockwise on alternate evenings, except when guest-nights fall on the second Thursday in the month, when it is passed clockwise. As it happened, it was on one of these Thursdays that the race relations monitor, Mr R. S. Viswamacharya, first appeared.

Although disappointed to find that nobody noticed his race or colour, he began gamely talking about anti-racist consciousness-raising and suchlike, and was still talking when it became his duty to pass the port. He passed it in the wrong direction, then, hearing his neighbours gasp, waited eagerly for a discriminatory "racist" thunderbolt to fall.

But Colonel Haggard was delighted by this opportunity to complicate the port-passing ritual still further. Ordering Mr V. to be supplied with a second decanter, he laid down that henceforth he would have the exclusive right to pass the port in both directions at the same time.

In his subtle Hindu mind Mr V. now found himself involved in serpentine speculations about the nature of time, space and indeed reality. Soon this learned Brahmin became as great an enthusiast for regimental custom as the Colonel himself. His "anti-racist" preoccupations, now seen as utterly trivial, dropped away. He is a man fulfilled. He has been promoted Honorary Major. And so the latest plot against the Yeomanry has come to nothing.

Ominous Spring

Driving from Cornwall across southern England in this retarded spring, we saw beech trees still in their fresh green beauty at the end of May; in the woods, almost a month late, swathes of bluebells; May blossom scarcely out; and on roadside banks, primroses and campions flowering together.

We hear customary grumbling about the weather, apprehensive rather than pleasurable ("they say it's been the coldest May since 1675"). But then "one hardly knows to whom to complain". In the pastures, under leaden skies of ill omen, herds of comely, healthy beasts, evidently gathered for slaughter, grazed or stood about, unconscious of their doom.

These innocent creatures of course, could have no knowledge in their knobbly skulls of the truth about that malign combination of politicians, scientists, agrotechnologists and poisoned food purveyors which has brought them — and us — to this dreadful pass. But then, in our own baffled, lie-crammed skulls, come to think of it, no more can we.

Crash Programme

The drink-driving limit in France, Belgium, Holland, Finland and Greece is now 50mg of alcohol per 100ml of blood; in Portugal, 40mg; in Sweden, 20mg. In Great Britain it is still 80mg, and needless to say there is a big campaign coming up to reduce it, supported by experts in all kinds of grotesque academic disciplines from behavioural science to "alcohol education". The eventual object, of course, is to make it illegal for drivers to drink alcohol at all.

But there is still a scandalous neglect of the pioneering research work of Dr Ron Hardware and his dedicated team of scientists at Nerdley University. Dr Hardware was the first to investigate "passive drinking" and put it on a proper scientific basis. He showed that the consumption of even a minute quantity of alcohol can *in certain conditions* affect everybody within a range of 10 miles.

Obviously this has important implications not only for the general health of the nation but also for drink-driving. A recent series of experiments at Nerdley showed that the presence of passengers who had consumed alcohol could have a measurable effect *even on a driver who had consumed none*.

In one experiment in a stationary car, with all four occupants, of course, wearing seatbelts, the driver was given no alcohol while the *front* passenger drank, over a period of 30 minutes, four large measures of brandy and ginger ale, four large vodkas and a standard bottle of white wine. After 20 minutes he was already showing noticeable effects. After 30 minutes he ripped off his seatbelt, began talking loudly in a tone described as "elated" and tried to sing, in an unmusical voice, several once popular songs ranging from *I belong tae Glesca* to *You'd be Far Better Off in a Home*. Finally, he slumped across the driver, gabbling "A man's best friend is his mother" in a maudlin tone and became semi-conscious, causing the driver to remove his hands from the wheel, while the two rear passengers showed secondary reactions ranging from "dismay" to "alarm" and "nervous joviality".

"It's clear," says Dr Hardware, "that if the car had been in motion, even at a low speed, the driver might have lost control and an accident, possibly serious, might have resulted. Admittedly, this was an extreme case. But we have shown under laboratory conditions, by inverse intropolation of all the relevant data, that the danger is present at all levels of alcohol intake."

When, Dr Hardware asks, is the Government going to act on these findings? When is it going to enforce drink tests not only for all drivers but for all passengers or, since almost everybody may be a passenger at one time or another, for the whole population at all times? And incidentally, when is it going to finance a massive crash programme of further research, with more facilities and personnel and new, bigger laboratories in an enlarged Nerdley Scientific Complex?

More! More!

"A few misguided people," said Paul Ohm, the Edgbaston freelance technologist, addressing a seminar of futurologists at Droitwich, "are grumbling about the proposal to introduce a new series of telephone codes, starting with the digit 02, only 16 months after the change to 01. But surely all progressive people welcome these changes.

"We need more of them. Personally I am in favour of changing the prefixes — and all the numbers, if feasible — every few months. It would also be good to change all phone numbers, not to seven or eight digits as now proposed, but to hundreds or thousands of digits.

"Remembering all those numbers would provide excellent training in basic numeracy, a capability more and more essential if this country is to keep up with its competitors in the race to the future. Having our heads full of numbers at all times will help us to shed the mental lumber — words, tunes, images, speculations, emotions and so on — which clogs our brains and prevents them from functioning with maximum efficiency.

"I am training myself to dream entirely in numbers, dispensing with all unnecessary dream material," he went on to prolonged applause, as his eyes began to revolve rapidly in opposite directions, his feet turned back to front and he levitated several feet in the air.

From the Moors

With the recession in demonstrations for big political causes, Rentacrowd, the mammoth consortium which supplies howling mobs for all occasions, now concentrates on smaller accounts such as animal rights and hunt sabotage. It has seldom had a more testing assignment than the demonstration by London Animal Action and the Hunt Saboteurs' Association outside the Savoy Hotel, where grouse flown from the moors on the Twelfth was on the menu.

"Scientists at our research division on the North Circular Road," says a spokesman, "were at full stretch for weeks programming these new semi-automated demonstrators. It was touch and go whether the state-of-the-art Foaming, Cat-calling Hunt Saboteur Mk II would be ready in time. Our backroom boys, working flat out on the intricate circuitry, were near despair."

In fact there was an explosion at the end of last month in a top secret laboratory, when clouds of evil-smelling smoke drifted over the neighbourhood and television screens were blacked out.

"There are still a few minor snags, headaches and teething troubles to be ironed out," the spokesman says. "One of the Animal Action models at the Savoy apparently malfunctioned when he tried to force his way inside to grab a helping of grouse for himself. But all's well that ends well."

"A disappointing Twelfth," reports *Blazeaway*. "But landowners who had the foresight to stock their moors with ecologist, conservationist and other breeds which do well on acid soils with plenty of torn-up pamphlets and old signposts report decent bags. I don't know whether roast conservationist was on the menu at the Savoy. Don't care for it myself, but there are those who says it's good eating with a béchamel sauce.

"As for roast hunt saboteur, I tried it once and, phew, once was quite enough, I can tell you."

Ancient Melodies

Abandoning a long-held rule, the Vienna Philharmonic Orchestra is taking on women players. I do not know whether this is due to the pressure of fashionable prejudice or to the predominance of women in music schools. One factor making for caution in Vienna must have been reports of the experience of women players in the old Stretchford Metropolitan County Symphony Orchestra under its veteran conductor Sir Jim Gastropodi.

The Poggibonsi-born maestro had all the traditional susceptibility and gallantry of his countrymen towards the fair sex. But that may have been one reason why he was chary of engaging women players, particularly attractive ones. Both Miss Hilda Tonks, for many years principal harpist, and her second Miss Vera Craggs, were of distinctly skeletal appearance. As for the two or three women second violins, they were often described by the more kind-hearted of Sir Jim's "lads" as "looking like the back of a cab".

This did not save them from vulgar catcalling, rude horseplay and worse. During one performance of Mahler's Symphony No 38 (the "Interminable") at the Sadcake Hall in the Seventies, those among the audience who were awake could observe a percussion player furtively using a bent wire taken from the mechanism of the tubular bells to draw Miss Tonks' handbag towards him and grab whatever small sums of cash it might contain.

A loud scream from the harpist and a shout of "Look out, Miss Tonks!" from a public-spirited concert-goer did not save her property. The rest of the orchestra, quickly covering up in male solidarity, began to play a quiet, subtly orchestrated passage of Mahler's four-hour-long slow movement fortissimo, while the percussive thief made his getaway. Gesticulating helplessly, Sir Jim fell off his podium and knocked himself out.

And at that moment Ron Spheroyd, the 24-stone principal bass tuba and Chief High Archimandrite of the District Basilica of the Musicians' Union (no humble "Father of the Chapel" for him), took up his instrument and blew the stupendous B Flat which signifies "All out!" He had always maintained that the presence of women players was a threat to his differentials, if not to the whole trade union movement, and this provocative behaviour of Miss Tonks, he thought, proved his point.

Survivors

H. G. Wells, the great writer of scientific romances and rationalist who at the last found himself facing *Mind at the End of its Tether*, died 50 years ago. Among the few still alive who knew him well must be the nonagenarian sisters Estelle and Anita Maclean-Gropius, both formidable Hampstead thinkers of the old school. Estelle was formerly Head of St Ulbricht's Anti-Colonialist Nursery School in Lumumba Gardens, where Bert Brecht Mao Che Banana, Mrs Dutt-Pauker's bearded little activist grandson, now aged 31, is still a pupil.

Anita was former Keeper of Graffiti at the Victoria and Albert Museum. She is the world's greatest authority on the Master of Paddington, whose lost *chef d'oeuvre* — *Far Away is Close at Hand in Images of Elsewhere* — has been restored on a wall outside his eponymous station. A new, revised edition of her great Catalogue Derangé of the Master's work (Viper and Bugloss, £495) has been chosen as Art Historical Book of the Year by her nephew and heir, the critic Roy Watson-Cronk.

The sisters have not been on speaking terms for 50 years. Each claims that the other was the only Fabian woman in Hampstead not to have been seduced by Wells; and each indignantly claims she was.

Two Faces

Glancing at a newspaper article (one of thousands appearing just now) on the "conflict between religion and science", I thought how aptly two contrasting photographs of their respective champions had been chosen. There on the one hand was Dr Richard Dawkins, the Oxford anti-religious scientist, with his smiling, boyish face, his well brushed yet becomingly untidy hair falling over a broad, intelligent brow, his casual shirt open at the neck, just as though he had come from an afternoon's practice at the nets, and a very satisfactory practice at that, to judge from his keen, frank and possibly blue-eyed gaze.

And there on the other hand was the old, lined, careworn face of Dr Runcie, the former archbishop, with his receding hair, his dark, baggy eyes behind thought-laden spectacles, his troubled mouth partly concealed by a hand bearing a heavy archiepiscopal ring. His sombrely clad body suggested worry, tension, sorrow and doubt.

"Which of these men," the headline asked, "knows more about what life means?" I am not sure what answer was expected. Most people, certainly, would prefer the man who knows more about life to be the happy-looking, confident Dawkins rather than the agonised and doubting Runcie. Yet what sort of answer, however attractive, would that be?

Beyond (and around) this sterile old debate there still howls and groans the same bad old world, just as it always has, whether created or evolved, the world real people live in, filled with grief and pain and injustice and redeemed only by individual goodness, human and divine. Which of these antagonists, the blithe scientist or the brooding churchman, looks as if he knows anything at all about that?

At Marxmount

One by one they go. Now Pavel Sudoplatov, once head of the special operations branch of the NKVD (later the KGB), responsible under Stalin for planning and supervising political assassinations — his greatest single achievement was the assassination of Trotsky — has left us at the age of 89.

The shadow of mortality falls over Mrs Dutt-Pauker, the great Hampstead thinker, as she sits in her study at Marxmount, her fine white house on the edge of the Heath, amid the trophies of a life devoted to the People's Struggle for peace and higher living standards: from the signed photograph of Stalin in its silver frame to the upper set of Bukharin's false teeth mounted in gold, a keepsake from old Stonebottom Molotov himself.

Dear Pavel! The Chatelaine of Marxmount thinks of those glorious days of the Thirties when, full of ardour and idealism, she went to Catalonia to help the People's Struggle against Franco. Not a few of the People's Champions fell for the fiery young upper-class English girl who had impulsively thrown in her lot with the Spanish People. Ernö Gerö, Josip Broz, Walther Ulbricht, and not least Pavel Sudoplatov himself sought her love beneath the velvet, star-studded night skies of Spain! Who cared about Spender and Auden when the lovely young Honourable Myrtle Templeton-Bagshaw was around?

For a time she was drawn to Pavel, whose methods of economising on ammunition when dealing with anarchists, syndicalists and other "rotten elements" strongly appealed to her romantic nature. But in the end it was Walther Ulbricht, later so prominent in building socialism in the German Democratic Republic, who won her heart with his handsome looks and fascinating plans for forced labour camps for enemies of the People, sadly abandoned when the Fascists triumphed and the heartbroken lovers had to part and carry on the struggle in their separate ways.

Memories, memories: what was Pavel's nickname for her in those old days in Barcelona? "The English Pasionaria?"! A flush suffused her withered Marxist cheek. How little she had deserved that honour! But after all, an English girl, however enthusiastic for the Cause, could hardly be expected to emulate the feat of the great Pasionaria by severing a priest's jugular with her teeth!

Yet she had done her best. She had not let her comrades down. When she pleaded, Walther had even let her sign the occasional death warrant. Now, when the task was to build socialism all over again, she would not give up the struggle. It was in this mood of mingled nostalgia and resolution that her daughter Deirdre, returning from a "Brits out of Ireland" demo, found her at her desk in the deepening twilight.

Deirdre's resemblance to the long-lost Walther, vestigial beard and all, struck her mother so powerfully that a tear welled from her dialectical eye and splashed on to her Gramscian blotter. How was Deirdre, so used to gruff dismissal, to know she owed the soft look her mother turned on her to news of an aged monster lately dead in far-off Moscow?

A Problem Solved

With the fall of South Africa and the end of statutory apartheid, well-meaning people in England may have thought that "racism" — for many of them the worst if not the only sin in the world — would simply fade away and all South Africans, equal at last, would live happily ever after. Things have not turned out like that. People of all races are still thinking and behaving like the incorrigible human beings most of them undoubtedly are.

The South African Human Rights Commission has drawn up an enormous programme to deal with this menace. All public and private institutions will be required to draw up an annual "racism audit", as legally valid as a financial one. An office of investigation will hold public inquiries into all manifestations of "racism". A national "racism barometer" will be established to measure the state of "anti-racism practice" everywhere.

Why are the South Africans ignoring advances in anti-racist technology? What need of barometers? Why aren't they using the racial prejudometer, the electronic device developed by the British Prejudo Consortium for the race relations industry? You have only to point this handy little instrument (it fits easily in pocket or handbag) at another person (or at yourself) and then read off the degree of prejudice in prejudons, the internationally recognised scientific unit of racial prejudice.

A large-scale version is being developed which can be installed in schools, offices, factories and public places to read off detailed statistics both of collective and individual prejudice, which can then be processed and collated by a central agency. When the prejudometer is used universally it will be possible for everybody to worry about the "problem of racism" not just occasionally, as now, but all the time.

A Wrong Righted

Klaus Hänsch, president of the European Parliament, is promising reform of its members' system of expenses. By working this, some of them are alleged to pocket two or three times their basic salaries. A recent television documentary, using a hidden camera, showed several signing on for their meals and accommodation allowance of £175 a day, then immediately going home.

But before the expense system is reformed, Herr Hänsch proposes to "harmonise" salaries for all the 626 MEPs. This is good news for British ones. At present they are paid the same salary, £42,000 a year, as Westminster MPs. This is about a quarter of what the Italians and Germans get.

Mr Jeremy Cardhouse, formerly MP for Stretchford North and leader of the Tories for Progress Group, now Socialist Euro-MP for the

Stretchford Conurbation, is delighted. "The disgracefully low pay of British Euro-MPs compared with some others has long cried out to heaven for vengeance," he says. "It is wonderful that this flagrant injustice is to be redressed at last.

"We British Euro-MPs are ashamed to look foreign Euro-MPs in the face. Some of them openly mock us as paupers and 'poor John Bulls'. Only the other day an Italian Euro-MP threw some lira coins of low denomination in my direction. When I bent down to pick them up he screamed with laughter and a big brute of a German Euro-MP aimed a kick at me from behind.

"No wonder some of us are tempted to recoup by claiming expenses to which we may not always be strictly entitled. I have never stooped to such practices myself. I have always been careful to sign for my own daily meals and accommodation allowance even when I could not be absolutely certain I would not be called home unexpectedly the next day. I have always claimed for airline travel in a conscientious way even though I might find later on that I did not have to make that particular journey after all.

"It will be a great relief when I am paid adequately and can hold up my head as a representative of Britain in the company of my foreign colleagues. What is almost as important, it will increase their respect for Britain. After all, what is good for my economy must be good for Britain's economy too. They are both part and parcel of the same great ongoing European process."

Believing, mistakenly, that his current idol Sir Leon Brittan had entered the European Parliament building, Mr Cardhouse went down on all fours and banged his head on the floor. Twisting round to smile in all directions, he suffered an attack of his old trouble, multiple convolvulitis. But before he was taken to hospital in considerable pain he managed heroically to sign an expense claim for meals and accommodation for that day and the whole of the week.

With the Nodules

The controversial new film *Jam*, about people who are sexually excited by traffic jams, has set off a tremendous row in the traffic jam fan community. *Traffic Jam*, the old-established fans' magazine, has called for the film's suppression ("Outrageous ... an insult to all traffic jam aficionados ... it is time to kick out the arty trendies and get back to motoring family values").

But *Snarl-Up*, which appeals to younger fans, says: "A literally blaz-

ing masterpiece of filmic art ... go and see it — now!" Seventy-six per
cent of readers agree.

A controversial article by "celebrity guest writer" the Rev John
Goodwheel, Chaplain-General to the Motorists' Liberation Front, takes
a surprisingly balanced view: "We of the MLF want to see an end to all
traffic jams. But until then, don't let's be judgmental. I believe that in
this day and age there's room for motorists of every automobilistic sexual
orientation in our multi-motoring community in a very real sense."

Harry and Janet Nodule, the well-known traffic jam fans of Brassgrove
Park, south London, are simply disgusted. They spent their honeymoon
in the Seventies in a legendary 25-mile jam on the old A30 near Exeter.
But both insist that "nothing nasty occurred".

The other day, as they were staring out of the window at their seven-
year-old Boggs Popular saloon waiting in the wintry street, and wondering whether to drive somewhere and find a good snarl-up for the rest of
the day, some lines gradually appeared on the upper part of the front of
Harry's head between the strips of hair above the two small apertures he
uses for seeing, and he suddenly said: "This — er — film."

"Yes, dear?" Janet said. "It might be — er — interesting to see it,"
said Harry. A kind of reddish patch spread slowly over the central part
of the front of Janet's head. "Oh Harry, how could you? I think you're
horrible! I never thought you were like that! Don't come near me!"
The corners of the horizontal aperture in the lower part of the front of
her head turned down and a sort of weak, strangled wailing noise came
out of it.

The globular protrusion at the front of the stretchable area which
connects Harry's head to his shoulders moved up and down gulpingly
several times. "Sorry, dear," he said at last. "It was only a thought. I
don't mean anything. Come along, dear, let's go and find a nice tailback
somewhere — I fancy the Croydon area today, don't know why — where
we can forget about the seamy side of life. They say it takes all sorts to
make a world, but don't worry, dear, we don't belong to it anyhow," he
went on soothingly, scratching the top of his head where it comes to a
marked point.

And soon a prolonged sniff from Janet showed he was forgiven.

Copybook Headings

Argument about the phenomenon of more and more badly-behaved, disruptive, even uncontrollable children and its causes is raging in the "media" between conventional moralists and progressive child-experts who,

though they will never admit it, also have their own conventional beliefs. A woman writer in the *Guardian* believes "the disintegration of parental authority is the result of the current profound change and uncertainty about the role of men and women in the family".

As a conventional feminist thinker she welcomes this, believing that the "old authoritarianism of the father" has gone for ever, together with "the structure that mirrored it, the patriarchal church and authoritarian school"; and good riddance to them all. "Families now have to make up the rules as they go along. This is no collapse of a moral order but the difficult birth of a new morality that tries to teach morality without fear."

What is this but a beguiling day-dream? To begin with, isn't the idea of a new morality by which men and women are held to be equal and to have an equal, shared role in the family still confined mainly to northwestern Europe and America, and even there found mainly in the restricted circles of a few comparatively prosperous, enlightened persons, many of them progressive journalists? Around them, in the wide world, the unregenerate masses of humankind still maintain the different roles of men and women and uphold as best they can the traditional structures of the family.

But could this "new morality" gradually come to prevail everywhere in a "new world order"? It is certainly possible to imagine quite large groups of people living by its light, behaving well themselves and bringing up children to behave well without fear. It is William Morris's dream of an ideal society in *News from Nowhere*, subsisting (after unspecified disturbances and revolutions) in an idyllic Thames Valley of the future, without any obvious connection with the outer world.

One does not like to be too gloomy and nasty about this. But wouldn't the unregenerate outer world eventually break in on these colonies of the enlightened with all the supposedly outmoded horrors of violence and war? Wouldn't the enlightened be compelled, in order to defend themselves, to summon up anew the old masculine and patriarchal virtues, or perish as many societies which tried to live without fear must have perished in the past?

Whatever Next?

Welcoming Mr Blair at the start of his preachifying visit to South Africa, Mr Mandela said: "I am not going to interfere in British politics, but the Labour Party supported us when the entire world was against us. We must not make the mistake of forgetting old friends."

It would be tasteless, perhaps even naff and common, to criticise this universally revered old gentleman. But on this occasion he does seem to have delivered himself of a most amazing lot of nonsense, doesn't he? Far from being against the efforts of Mr Mandela and his friends to over-throw the then existing order in South Africa, the entire world — at any rate the entire politically liberal, respectable and vocal part of it — was unreservedly on his side. "I yield to no one in my abhorrence of apart-heid"; wasn't this an obligatory mantra for anybody speaking about South Africa, from Mrs Thatcher to the humblest sports official?

Has he forgotten the enforced resignation of South Africa from the United Nations; the United Nations' trade sanctions against her; the worldwide efforts of the anti-apartheid industry — not least in this country — the pickets, the marches, the demonstrations, the persecution of South African grapefruit and lady bowls players; the devious channelling of funds to the ANC; the financial pressures; the continual threats of pain and ruin from the Bar of World Opinion?

Has he forgotten how the Communist Empires helped to train black revolutionaries in the "front-line states"; how they supplied arms for the terrorist war in Rhodesia, an essential preliminary to the planned attack on South Africa itself? Without all this, where would Mr Mandela be now? Ingratitude on this scale, unless due to clinical amnesia, is awe-inspiring.

Correspondence

Sir — Thanks to the dedicated work of American geneticists and biochemists, processed foods incorporating GMOs — genetically modified organisms — I am obliged to simplify — will soon be appearing on our supermarket shelves. You would think the benefits of this new food technology, which has produced essential articles of our diet like soya beans and sweetcorn cheaply and conveniently, would be obvious to all.

But already the Luddite parrot-cries of "wicked genetic engineer-ing", "interfering with Nature", "Frankenstein" and all the rest of it have been raised. Supermarkets are being forced to label food containing GMOs so that customers can avoid them. This is merely pandering to ignorance and superstition. It is also futile, since more and more food will contain GMOs as the technology of genetic engineering advances, whether stupid British consumers like it or not.

Any way why should any reasonable person object? If there is any danger of poisoning, disease or giving birth to deformed babies from the new products, surely that is a small price to pay for scientific advances.

This outcry is part of an ungrateful, reactionary movement against science and technology which is making this country a desert where scientists are cowering in caves, terrified for their lives.

I have already been subject to abuse and physical attack (pelting with so-called "organic" vegetables etc.) because of my genetic engineering experiments: e.g. my production of a new type of electronic bread, enriched with GMOs, which turns into toast on a voiced command.

Paul Ohm

Atomdene, Edgbaston

Birdbath's Christmas

There was dense fog on the Derbyshire uplands as Mr Shuttleworth, poultry farmer, part-time literary agent and Julian Birdbath's closest neighbour, shambled cursing over the stony ground to deliver Christmas mail to the Last Citizen of the Republic of Letters, who was toiling asway at his projected Life of Stephen Spender in his last refuge amid the murk and gloom of No 3 Level, Deadwater Leadmine (disused), near Bakewell.

"A Merry Christmas, lad, doubled-ended, zinc-bottomed and with copper knobs on!" was Shuttleworth's cheery greeting. He tipped a mass of sodden paper — news cuttings, old reviews, obsolete Christmas cards, the odd paperback copy of essays by Charles Lamb or Oliver Wendell Holmes — down the shaft on to the bowed head of the man who once, in a famous feat of literary detection, had discovered the so-called "missing Brontë brother", Dwight.

Birdbath's head sank onto his rusting typewriter and he fell into a troubled dream. He was standing, alone, in the midst of a glittering literary party where figures from the past and present seemed to mingle strangely together. Now he was addressing Cyril Connolly with a polite inquiry, only to find himself peering at Salman Rushdie's unfriendly beard. Now Geoffrey Grigson snatched away his canapé with a contemptuous sneer, then merged into a haughty Martin Amis and, the next second, horse-faced Louis MacNeice.

An unearthly light illumined the distant hair of Melvyn Bragg; Virginia Woolf turned pale. For a moment he thought he saw Carmen Callil smiling at him enchantingly from a far corner. Then a mouse sprang from her mouth and suddenly all was shadow as a portentous voice proclaimed: "Birdbath, thou art weighed in the balance and found wanting." He woke, his mind clouded with a terrible sense of unreality, to find Amiel, his pet toad and sole companion, well-meaningly trying to decorate his mouldering desk with chewed-up red-and-black typewriter ribbons.

Groaning, the doomed author reached for his diary and entered: "Angstometer reading: 276.8 — is this a record?" Far off, in the dim recesses of the mine, a rusting spar fell from an old pit-cage, its melancholy clang mingling with the drip of water and the tinkle of stalactites in a weird and dismal symphony.

Ecumenical Days

Dr Spacely-Trellis, the go-ahead Bishop of Bevindon, welcomes the 30 new mosques to be built in his diocese between now and the Millennium. "It is a heartening pledge of commitment to bridge-building between the communities, a shining witness to the multi-faith vision which underpins the religious mindset of all men and women of goodwill today in a very real sense," he says.

To set an example, he has offered the south transept of the newly rebuilt Bevindon Cathedral, a striking glass and concrete structure designed by the neo-post-brutalist architect, Sir Jeff Dreadbolt, to the Muslims for use as a mosque. There are also many redundant churches in his diocese, now crumbling away and boarded up against the depredations of the owl, bat and vandal, which could be made available to Hindus and Buddhists, particularly those of the Tantric sect, which has made many converts among young people in the Stretchford conurbation.

Dr Trellis believes that animists and pagans of various kinds must also be catered for. He is interested in the environmentally correct Yanomani Indians of the Amazon forest, popular among the bead-infested, natural-oil-crazed boutique owners of the picturesque, tourist-inveigling Lampton Road district of Nerdley. On the recent visit he good-humouredly showed his skill with the ecological blowpipe and got a big laugh when one of his darts (guaranteed environmental and non-poisonous) narrowly missed a passing policeman.

The influential Aztec community in Nerdley, descended from the Aztecs, who are believed to have colonised the neighbourhood in the so-called "Dark Ages" after crossing the Atlantic in stone boats, are demanding a prominent place in the Bishop's plans.

"Any attempt to exclude us will be regarded as a typical racist provocation in the context of the people's struggle and met with merciless rigour," stated one of their leaders, 44-year-old South Shields-born Royston Huitzilopochtli (formerly Royston Vibes), a 24th-year sociology student at Nerdley University.

Dr Trellis suggests that, a an ecumenical gesture, one of his retired clergy, 83-year-old Prebendary Aylwin Sheep-Harris, should offer himself for sacrifice on the new Aztec step-pyramid outside the former Nerdley Public Library. But a police spokesman stated: "Without wishing to prejudge the issue or offer offence to an ethnic minority, we would point out that human sacrifice has not yet been legalised in this country."

At a meeting of a new organisation, Football Managers for a Multi-Faith Millennium, Dr Trellis said he was "dead chuffed and over the moon". But his domestic chaplain, the Rev. Peter Nordwestdeutscher, winced painfully at his affected language. and even the Bishop's "partner", Mantissa Shout, the former militant deaconess and fearless activist for women's ordination, hastily drew her smart black "Muslim-type" silk headscarf over her face.

An Expert View

A television programme about day-care centres for children is said, truly for all I know, to have set off a great argument among experts about whether putting children in them while their mothers go to work is good or bad for their future health and education.

At a weekend seminar at Droitwich, Dr Heinz Kiosk, the well-known social psychologist and chief psychiatric adviser to the Food Safety Authority, said he had no doubt about the matter:

"It is amazing that any responsible person nowadays can dispute that child-care centres are vastly superior to mothers as an influence on young children. Apart from enabling mothers to work, and thus make a meaningful contribution to our social and economic progress, they can instil, at a very early age, the essential values of our society in an efficient way. People who have no other claim on children than a so-called maternal relationship can never hope to do this.

"Instead of dealing in trivial personal feelings and opinions, all too often based on outmoded superstition and ignorance, day-care centres can systematically inculcate essential democratic and humanist values in small children. They can stress sexual and racial equality, root out undesirable, discriminatory attitudes such as homophobia, and emphasise the importance of human rights and universal sex education.

"We are all agreed, I think, that day-care centres, provided they are run by people with the right ideas and attitudes, are the key to adult health and educational standards. But two things are needed: to make them compulsory for all children, whether their mothers are working or not; and to make all children attend them from the earliest possible age.

"I would favour six months or even earlier. There is no reason in principle why mothers, whose influence is often reactionary and pernicious, should have access to their children at all until day-care centres have set them firmly on the right path.

"Until our society shows this proper concern for children it will remain a guilty society. And it is not only society which is guilty," he shouted, as his audience, scraping back their chairs, began, too late, a panic-stricken rush for doors and windows, "WE ARE ALL GUILTY!"

Oh, All Right

In our dull and dimwit age, everything has to be politicised. Here is part of a notice in the *Independent* about a production, at a new theatre in Belfast, of Synge's *Playboy of the Western World*: "An odd choice of opener hereabouts: the world of agricultural poverty and social deprivation the play represents, you might argue, was all down to the British and the post-Famine Anglo-Irish landowners..."

As Synge, Yeats and Lady Gregory often used to bellow in unison at those discussion meetings they were fond of attending on such topics as "Towards a Socialist Ireland": "Brits Out! Out! Out! Out!"

Canine Arts

In London a yellow labrador has opened an exhibition of sculptures, costing as much as £500 each, which she has chewed up and moulded from various raw materials. In their youth, our own two yellow labradors — the late beautiful and high-spirited Rosie and her beautiful though less ebullient daughter Daisy, who still survives — both proved artistically gifted. But they never had an exhibition or sought to make money from their art, or threatened to bite Mr Serota if he did not put their sculptures in the Tate Gallery.

They were very selective in their choice of materials. The only works surviving from their earliest period are finely chewed chair legs. But in their middle period, their preference was for chewing books; not all books by any means, but books that seemed to make a relevant, meaningful, even committed statement about the canine predicament in the age of the transvaluation of all values.

They began with books about dogs or dog training, then, tiring of these, switched to cookery books, and then, in their later post-destructionist period, began chewing up copies of Shakespearean plays before giving up their art altogether. A notable work by Daisy, who was Westmorland-bred on her father's side, was chewing up a book on the topography of Buckinghamshire, on loan from the London Library.

The library's rule is that a damaged book must be replaced or its value made good. But when I wrote to explain that a labrador dog had been responsible and that I had told her not to chew up any more London Library books, all was forgiven. There is a moral here; but not all, by any means, will find it to their taste.

Votes for Nobody

There is a proposal that mayors, even lord mayors, should be elected – whether by councillors, ratepayers, registered voters or popular acclamation, is yet uncertain. Most people will be wondering what Alderman Foodbotham, the 25-stone, crag-jawed, iron-watch-chained, grim-booted perpetual chairman of the Bradford City Tramways and Fine Arts Committee in the great days, and for many years Lord Mayor, would have thought of this thoroughly democratic idea.

If the Great Alderman had been willing, in his accustomed phrase, to "take cognisance" of it at all, he would soon have shown in words which might have shaken his own town hall from its foundations to its soot-blackened, bell-booming towers, that his view of the office of mayor was quite different from any held at all commonly today.

His own majestic eminence, of course, would have ensured his election, if there had been elections, by any conceivable method of suffrage. Over the councillors his authority was absolute. The common people held him in total veneration. But he held strongly that they neither ought to have nor wished to have any voice in local government whatsoever.

It was for them to tremble and obey. Apart from a few malcontents and hangdog levellers, easily dealt with by traditional methods such as fearful grimacing or confinement to the municipal dungeons, they were perfectly ready to do so. It was not for these humble, loyal folk, Foodbotham believed, when in their brief hours of ease from toil in his stupendous mills they supped mugs of ale or, more commonly, cups of ipecacuanha or sarsaparilla over a harmless game of dominoes or ludo, to speculate on the affairs of the mighty.

It was their privilege, in fugitive moments, to find their lives irradiated by a sense of awful mystery at the mere thought of other worlds than theirs, and to offer — it was all they had — the tribute of a simple smile of gratitude and wonder. As for Foodbotham himself, he always used to say: "A place for every man and every man in his place." And for emphasis he would settle his majestic bottom even more firmly in his chairman's seat while the Town Hall chamber rang to the applause of brow-beaten councillors and assorted sycophants.

Clones of Destiny

The "genetic revolution", which now offers the possibility of cloning human beings, is beginning to worry scientists themselves. No wonder: even the first cloned sheep has a strangely evil, unsheeplike look about it. "Science has placed in Man's hands innumerable gifts which he can use either for good or ill": this familiar old mantra is not heard so often nowadays, no doubt because of the preponderance of ill is becoming obvious even to fervent admirers of Man's relentlessly generous and insistent friend.

That grotesquely named body, the Human Fertilisation and Embryology Authority, may seek laws to bring this latest gift of science under its control. Prof Joseph Rotblat, a scientist whose warning voice is often heard, calls for an "international ethical committee to control the work of scientists in sensitive areas". He thinks that "new means of mass destruction, perhaps more readily available than nuclear weapons", may be on the way.

But all experience shows that whatever scientists can discover will be exploited, and that whatever laws may be enacted to forbid its development it will still be developed. The progress of science and technology seems to be something *fated*. Neither "Man" nor "we" nor any of the other shadowy agencies so often called upon to "choose", seem to have the smallest power to do so.

Only a new Inquisition, a thousand times more powerful than that old Inquisition now so unthinkingly condemned, could bring this process — after all, it is what we still call "Progress" — to an end. Unless, which is far more likely, it progresses to a stupendous, cataclysmic end itself.

Your TV Tonight

The Tubers: GPI Network, 6.30-7.00: When Jon Strongitharm, thirtyish ex-commando, paralibrarian and mystery man, moved into the Old Bell Foundry to write, as he claims, a blockbusting novel, he set all hearts in the Grumbridge Short Story Writing Circle aflutter. But is his immediate interest in Fiona and her mobile sex aid 'n' antique shop purely professional? Is her trip to Bosnia still on, in spite of the *fatwa* pronounced by popular Muslim vets Tim and Frank Sidiqi? Will Jon intervene, risking accusations of racism?

Tom's exhibition of Brussels sprout sculpture at the village arts centre has been vetoed by the "phantom environmental health officer". Will glamorous farmer/art critic Nick Barometer save the day? When the drama society stages a first performance of *Tess of the Nibelungs* with Elspeth in the name part, old Eva Tuber, leader of the militant senile delinquent faction at the Manor's old folks' home, closes it down by setting the village hall on fire. Will the Vicar enlist her, together with her nuclear-powered vacuum cleaner, as "research assistant" for his experiments on the ultimate building blocks of matter? And will the Colonel's threat to "sort things out" by using his Crimean War cannon to bombard the village with his hyper-vindaloo meatballs and mega-poppadums lead to an unexpected denouement?

Ofhunt

Even if hunting for pleasure is banned, packs of foxhounds could be licensed to control foxes, says Dr Cunningham, the new Minister for Agriculture, tactfully. He sits for the Copeland constituency in Cumberland, where two very popular foot packs hunt the rough fell country.

Hunting people accuse him of approving hunting "as long as those who take part in it don't wear red coats or ride thoroughbred horses or enjoy it". This is certainly the root of opposition to hunting among the big packs of progressive thinkers. But why, if hounds were licensed, shouldn't hunting people still follow them on thoroughbred horses, wear red coats, and enjoy the sport just the same? Could the *enjoyment* be made illegal?

The licensing of hounds would call for a new statutory body called Ofhunt or some such Soviet-style name. Ofhunt officials would accompany all hunts. It would be up to them to make sure that people did not enjoy them. They could ride on donkeys themselves, wear their office suits and grumble incessantly at the stupidity and danger of it all.

But some officials might find they enjoyed it and take to wearing red coats and riding thoroughbred horses at the public expense, maintaining, with their new-found hero Jorrocks, that any time not spent hunting foxes is a pointless waste.

A Child's Dream

"Steeped in the medium, Mr Jackson is claimed to have played at being a TV scheduler as a child. He stunned colleague in meetings with his encyclopaedic knowledge of the transmission times of the children's programme *Skippy* in the 1960s." This account of Michael Jackson, the new chief executive of Channel 4, made me reel back in dismay, my blood froze and for a moment I lost consciousness.

Yet there can be no more fitting chief of this monstrous agency than the man who was once that strange child.

As he played in the nursery with his schedules, did he stick to actually existing programmes or did he, with horrifying precocity, make up imaginary programmes of his own, even more moronic and infamous, palely foreshadowing the demonic achievements of today?

Have those who must have watched that child's appalling play in helpless alarm survived into a world where he has power to turn his childish dreams into terrible reality? Therein lies some hope. This example may have set them against watching television for life.

Again, this adult chief executive may still be fixated on the pleasures of his nightmare childhood. Every day we psychiatrists are meeting such cases. He may find himself so engrossed in pure scheduling — scheduling for its own sake — that he will make sure no actual programmes are ever transmitted at all. What a blessing that would be!

What the Papers Say

In a thoughtful leader, *The Feudal Times and Reactionary Herald* discusses Lord Archer's Succession to the Throne Bill, which would abolish the precedence of male heirs over female: "This measure is thoroughly pernicious both in itself and in its implications.

"It is only too fitting that its proposer is not only a 'life peer' — one of a whole class of chimerical persons — but is also, we understand, a writer of fiction designed for the perusal of the less thoughtful among the humbler classes.

"Should any of our readers, however, chance to find specimens of his trash in the hands of their servants, they may rest assured that it is at any rate trash of a comparatively harmless kind, likely to injure minds rather than morals.

"It is possible that the author, who belongs to the so-called 'Conservative' Parliamentary faction, but whose Bill, needless to say, is supported by the equally mis-named 'Labour' faction, intends some kind of sop to the mob of foaming radicals, envy ridden levellers and malcontent school-teachers at present agitating for the 'reform' of the Lords and the abandonment of that Hereditary Principle which is still one of our last remaining safeguards against ultimate chaos and darkness.

"At least this Bill offers no direct threat to the Hereditary Principle itself. Yet it is scarcely less pernicious for that. It promotes — and for whatever reason seems intended to promote — that fatal tendency towards 'sexual equality', the very hallmark of decadence, which we see advancing on every side.

"We see it advancing in daily life, in art and commerce, in the Church, even in the Armed Forces of the Crown, ensnaring even superior minds with false and sophistical arguments. We see, with unspeakable horror, how the gentler sex itself is being seduced, by all the arts of low-bred blandishment, to emulate the most coarse and brutal aspects of male behaviour, which it should be the task of true womanhood to soften and ameliorate.

"We may be sure that the commercial and financial interest now aggrandised and elevated to overweening power, will everywhere endeavour to pervert and deny the natural distinction between the sexes and turn both men and women into equally degraded and indistinguishable androgynes, the more easily to draw them all into its worldwide pandemoniac empire. Here is a new, seemingly almost inexpugnable force for universal slavery, to be imposed, needless to say, in the false name of human freedom.

"Can this literally infernal tendency prevail? Whatever the condition of the middling sort, ever open to be misled by novel and insubstantial notions, we must surely trust that there is still a bedrock of good sense among the decent, honest people of England which attaches them firmly to the proper distinction of the sexes and the proper place of woman as wife, mother and guardian of the family. If we are wrong, what hope remains?"

Ever Onwards

Stretchford University, which already has Visiting Professors of Road Rage Studies and Fat Cat Studies as part of its Department of Social Problematology, has appointed a Visiting Professor of Alcopop Studies. He is Dr Mike Gumbs, a graduate of media studies at the sister University of Lampton-on-Hoke (formerly St Oick's Polytechnic).

He is a tall, thin, pale-faced man who yet looks bloated, perhaps from the quantity of alcopops he consumes in the course of research. His breath smells strongly of newsprint and he has a rather foolish expression.

"Alcopops are my life," he says. "I don't mean I'm addicted to them. Far from it. But I'm concerned with every aspect of alcopops — their innumerable flavours, methods of consumption, whether by swig or straw, you name it — as key factor both in teenage culture and in the development of social problematological studies today.

"I see myself as something of a pioneer." He lowered his eyes modestly, then, suddenly opening them with a deft movement of thumb and forefinger, made them positively blaze with vacancy.

"I believe that, in a year's time, every university worthy of the name will have a Visiting Professor of Alcopop Studies presiding over a meaningful, relevant, vibrant powerhouse of academic research."

If Only

Was the great rally of country people in London really about foxhunting or even about the disappearing countryside? One noticeable thing was that the participants were all unmistakably English (a few came from Scotland and Wales, but no matter).

Some commentators have seen in this great gathering a rebirth of the Conservative Party. But these people, who were protesting against the threat to what, I suppose, we must call their "way of life", belonged to no particular political party. They know well enough by now that none of the existing parties will defend them. Something deeper than "democracy" is stirring here.

There has been much quoting of Chesterton's *"We are the people of England, that never have spoken yet"*, bringing a mournful thrill to the nostalgically inclined and drawing nasty sneers and insinuations of "fascism" from the smart nitpickers of the Left.

Are the people of England — not only the country people who gathered in Hyde Park, but all the English people dispossessed and threatened by creeping totalitarian socialism and the movement towards a New World Order — are they really trying to speak at last?

In the past 50 years they have seen everything that is distinctively English suppressed and derided. They have seen all the evils that flow from the gutters of America — vile entertainment, degenerate pop music, feminism, "political correctness" — infect their country.

They have seen their decent manners and customs corrupted. They have seen sexual deviance elevated in official esteem and even officially commended. They have seen parts of their country colonised by immigrants and been forbidden by law to speak freely of the consequences.

All this, they have suffered and have not spoken yet. If they are going to speak now, they have left it very late. Unlikelier things have happened in the past, but not many.

Dynasty

Trevor Gumbs, who teaches English at Bog Lane School in Stretchford, may be one of the first victims of the Blunkett Terror, under which unsatisfactory teachers can be sacked with four weeks' notice. "Big deal," says Trevor. He has already been offered a post as Reader in Rave Studies at Nerdley University, in the Department of Educational Sabotage and Applied Vandalism under Prof Wendy Dutt-Pauker, niece of the great Hampstead thinker. There he will be able to continue his own Long March through the Institutions more effectively than ever.

Trevor has a distinguished academic record. He holds a medal for conspicuous gallantry in the campaign against educational reform, won when, in a now legendary encounter, he jeered at Mr Blunkett even more raucously than any of the other activist teachers. He even made a horrible face at Mr Blunkett's fascist reactionary guide-dog.

Like his cousin Mike Grumbs, recently appointed Visiting Professor of Alcopop Studies at the University of Lampton-on-Hoke, in the Social Problematology Department run by Professor Pixie Dutt-Pauker, Wendy's sister, he belongs to the great Gumbs family, an intellectual dynasty that is the modern counterpart of the famous intellectual dynasties of the past century, the Trevelyans, Huxleys, Darwins and so on.

Only, of course, it is far superior to those, more truly relevant to our own time. It is "a People's Intellectual Dynasty", down to earth, entirely free of élitism, sharing in the life of the People as those stuffy upper and middle class Victorians, with their servants, inherited money (all based on the slave trade), country houses and gentlemen's clubs, could never hope to do.

Trevor's father, Stan Gumbs, a lifelong member of the Communist Party, was at one time director of the Ewan MacColl Foundation, supplying material for the Rentacrowd Workers' Folksong Factory, which in its heyday turned out as many as 5,000 workers' folksongs a year.

Stan's father, Frank Gumbs, was the great-grandson of the founder of the dynasty, Ebenezer Robespierre O'Brien Gumbs., the great revolutionary hero who is said to have signed the Chartist Petition of 1848 no fewer than 2,000 times in different names, his finest achievement in a long life devoted to the service of the People.

There are several members of this powerful intellectual clan at the BBC, working on the great task of eliminating any remaining traces of white, male, middle class, heterosexual influence from that institution and making it what its founders always meant it to be: a temple of pop art and communication on a level that the most multi-cultural, multi-sexual, multi-illiterate citizen of modern Britain can readily accept.

Spin

A news report casually mentioned that "senior spin doctors" — not any old spin doctors, you see — in the Labour Party were manipulating the news. At this rate "spin doctors" will soon become a recognised profession to be entered on passports or tax returns, as respectable as "pimp" or "conman".

News has always been spun. But spinning it systematically for the wholesale hoodwinking and confusion of the public depends on having a large quantity of news to spin. In former times there wasn't all that much news available. Except at times of crisis, people mostly got on with their own lives without being plagued by a continual, confused buzz of information about events in every part of the world which might be true or false.

Now, thanks to the "media", particularly television, the amount of news has become almost unlimited, and so has the will and power to spin. This may have an unforeseen consequence. Now that everybody has heard of spin doctors, they may begin to believe that all the news they hear is spun, and a cover-up for something else.

In the end they may stop believing in the news at all and take to minding their own business. Would that be a good thing or a bad thing?

New Model Army

At a weekend seminar at Woodhall Spa, Dr Heinz Kiosk, the eminent social psychologist and chief psychiatric adviser to the Meringue, Éclair and Profiterole Authority, spoke about Army reform: "We must, of course, rid ourselves of the current idea of the army as merely a body for making war to defend the state or engaging in other forms of institutionalised violence.

"If the Army is to have a proper place in our society its primary role must be to embody the values of that society, not necessarily as it is now, but as it ought to be. That is, the Army must be completely free of class, race or gender discrimination. For the interim period, however, we shall have to retain some kind of ranking system, if only to undo the present unjust arrangements.

"Positive discrimination will ensure that women, members of the ethnic minorities and the mentally and physically handicapped serve in the highest ranks and the present privileged classes — white, middle class public school products and the most intelligent and physically fit — in the lowest.

"Role-playing exercises with continual changes of rank can help eliminate pernicious ideas of continuity, 'tradition', 'smartness', 'discipline' and so on, which now prevent the Army from being an organic part of the equal society we are trying to build. An Army without 'discipline' would have an immense appeal for the young. Recruiting figures would shoot up to the astonishment of the most purblind 'Blimp'!

"We would soon have an Army which instead of being a laughing stock among social psychologists would represent our society as our present antiquated, tradition-ridden Army completely fails to do. Moreover, it would offer an example to the rest of the world, which I believe would take full advantage of it.

"Until we have such an Army, our society will be a guilty society. But," — his panic-stricken audience began scrambling too late for the doors and windows as his eyes began to revolve wildly in his head and he bellowed: "WE ARE ALL GUILTY!"

A Sad Business

English cricket, says the chairman of the England and Wales Cricket Board, is "no longer a force in the world". He favours various changes; fewer first-class county matches, more one-day matches, amalgamation of old local cricket leagues in a national structure, a national trophy ("an FA Cup for cricket") and other means of finally bringing English cricket down to the condition of football or American baseball — just another victim of the ravening spirit of democracy.

Why should English cricket be a "force in the world" anyhow? Is it because without being a force in the world it will never make enough money to enable professional cricketers to parade in vulgar opulence and delight the "media" with sensationally vile behaviour

Unless it is a force in the world, can there ever be up-to-date cricket managers to buy and sell players for enormous sums, enjoy picturesque nervous breakdowns or pronounce on the human predicament with proper doom-laden fatuity?

The sad decline of cricket began when professionals as well as amateurs started to have their initials on scorecards and use the same changing rooms. The great Lord Hawke, who was president of the Yorkshire County Cricket Club in the days when it invariably won the county championship, once said he would rather see the whole team dead at his feet than appoint a professional captain. Yes, he foresuffered and foresaw it all.

Even the fun-communists of the Thirties realised that cricket doesn't go with money-making: "If you want cricket, you'd better join us" (W. H. Auden).

An Ordinary Day

Sand, believed to have come from Spain, fell on Loftus Road, Nerdley, today, causing traffic hold-ups and delaying milk deliveries. Residents complained that several people, described as of "swarthy complexion", had also fallen.

"I found one in my garden, digging up my flowerbeds," said housewife Mrs Jean Dampbell, 52. "When I questioned him, he made no reply but rose rapidly into the air and disappeared over the neighbouring minimarket.

"They ought to do something about this, or these Spaniards will be everywhere, getting under our feet and upsetting the even tenor of what used to be a pleasant neighbourhood with nicely-spoken, law-abiding people.

"I didn't vote Labour for things like this," she added, as counsellors from Nerdley social services drove up in a van and offered a wide range of comforts from caring hugs to free tickets for a performance of the Marylous Ogreburg People's Bread and Marmite Street Dance Theatre on the following day.

A police spokesman stated later: "There was no racial element in this incident. It was probably just high spirits in the run-up to the August Bank Holiday." (*Nerdley Evening News*)

Idealist

Amid all the shock horror over schoolgirl mothers, Dr Llewelyn Goth-Jones, the director of community medicine for Stretchford, remains optimistic. "After all," he says, "it cannot be a bad thing for girls and boys to become sexually active as early as possible and take their proper place in our liberal society today. This will be even more important in the society of the future, when, I hope, sex at all times and with as many partners as possible will be the norm for everybody, whatever their age.

"Harmful, unhealthy concepts like 'childhood' and 'innocence', relics of past ages of repression, are the real problem. The best way to get rid of them, of course, is more and more sex education.

"As puberty — rather a suspect term in itself — arrives earlier and earlier, so schools will have to accustom pupils earlier and earlier to the use of condoms and the techniques of sex in all its variants.

"I look forward to a time when kids in nursery schools enjoy the benefits of sex education at six months or even earlier. My ultimate dream is sex education before birth. At our present rate of scientific progress and ever-increasing sex awareness it cannot be long before we have a breakthrough in that area. I call it "the last frontier".

"Of course, when all kids become sexually active, as they should, as soon as they are pubescent or before, then a certain number of girls are bound to become pregnant. Close supervision by teachers competent to apply the lessons of sex education to their pupils at first hand should gradually eliminate most of these cases.

"But to achieve the fully condom-conscious society we are trying to build, the Government must supply unlimited free condoms not only to schoolkids but to people of all ages, and set up a dedicated corps of experts to instruct everybody in their use. Prudes and reactionaries may complain. But I am proud to say I am one of those who have faith in the future."

As well as being director of community medicine, Dr Goth-Jones runs a chain of contraceptive advice centres, abortion clinics and "adult" cinemas in the West Midlands. He also operates a "fun sex" bus company in seaside towns in the summer. He is the star of a popular sex talk-in programme on GPI television, *Calling Dr Llew*. He is a director of an important subsidiary of the giant Nadirco Consortium, Malebolge Pharmaceuticals, which since it switched to mass condom production is enjoying a record-breaking boom.

No Fun at All

"Holidaying in occupied Cyprus is the moral equivalent of cheering on the Orangemen as they march down the Garvaghy Road," says a reader's letter in the *Independent*, always a rich mine of historical misinformation.

The writer is a Greek lady from Cambridge, and so may be excused. But the letter is interesting as a grotesque example of received opinion about the Ulster Unionists. English people who have never heard of the Turkish invasion of Cyprus and think Turkey is in North America will know one thing for sure: that Orangemen are brutal oppressors.

For a long time now the Ulster Unionists have had a very bad press over here. Whereas the southern Irish are seen as amiable (if sometimes undependable), intelligent, amusing and full of the joys of life, the Unionists are seen as gloomy, stupid, bigoted and boring. *They aren't fun*, you see. They produce comparatively few eminent pop singers, hairdressers, television cooks, homosexual dress designers, rubbish artists and esteemed fun people in general.

Their reputation for honesty, old-fashioned decency and respectability does them no good at all in the eyes of modish people in Britain. They are also guilty of another tendency unfashionable in this country; they defend themselves against their enemies. What would they have to do to redeem themselves from all this disgrace and win the good opinion of the massed fun-people of Britain? Ought they to give up all the Orange marches for good and put on a "gay pride" parade down the Garvaghy Road?

Vote No

As for Welsh devolution, the next item on the Blairite menu, I shall risk the columnar "kiss of death effect" and advise the Welsh people to vote against it. The only political party I have ever been a card-carrying member of is the Welsh Nationalist Party. But that was long ago, in the days when the great Saunders Lewis, the hero of Llyn, was its admirably reactionary leader.

Since then Plaid Cymru has gradually shed the reactionary ideas which, together with my love of the Welsh language, made it attractive to me. It has become decidedly Leftish, babbling boringly of democracy, economic affairs, the United Nations and the Great Fraud, "Europe", in which, as it pathetically hopes, an independent Wales would find its proper place at last.

It was not for this that King Arthur fought the Saxon and Merlin wove his spells and Blodwen Slagheap lured the elders from Capel Sion. Welsh self-rule would ensure that the most odious people in Wales — po-faced bureaucrats, greedy, squinting councillors and sly committee men — would dominate it.

As their smart new assembly led it further into that all-devouring "modern world" which is so profoundly un-Welsh, Wales would become not less but more like England. It would not be the noble tongue of Dafydd ap Gwilym which would prevail, but the sanitised, job-prodigal tongue of the bilingual car licence forms. Better by far to revive the ancient princedoms, with Gwynedd, the heartland of Welsh Wales, withdrawing into itself, with a Prince, not a President, as Head of State.

Would the greatest living Welshman, the poet R.S.Thomas, agree, however cantankerously, to accept the crown? In that narrow space he might create the reactionary paradise of my foolish dreams. The trunk roads, the power stations, the industrial estates, the tourist-infested theme parks — all will vanish like the false enchantments in the Mabinogion, and the only sounds amid that great blessed quietness will be the bleating of sheep and the declamations of the bards. And at his princely court not one word of English will be spoken.

No Vote

There will be no referendum on devolution for Cornwall, nor is there likely to be one, for all the efforts of Mebyon Kernow, the nationalist party, and a modest revival of the Cornish language, whose last native speaker died 200 years ago. To add insult to injury, Cornwall, far from getting separate treatment, is fated to be merely one of the seven south-western counties for which a mundane "regional development agency" is planned.

A universal nationalist, I had some correspondence with Cornish nationalists many years ago. At that time there were two nationalist parties, mutually hostile. One of them seemed to have been infiltrated by Marxists — they never let up, did they? — who were hot on English cultural imperialism, alienation and bungaloid fascism.

It must have been uphill work for them. But I have often thought, when sitting in some unfamiliar Cornish pub, that all would be perfect if the locals were chattering away in their own language, as in Wales, about the grotesque appearance and absurd affectations of English visitors, utterly confident that no-one could possibly understand a word of what they were saying.

It was not to be. My correspondents, I noticed, tended to have un-Cornish names like Sutcliffe and Marsden. They must have been the descendants of West Riding people who had retired to what they thought an earthly paradise beside the western sea. As with bigger and nastier nationalist movements, it is often those who are only partly of native blood, or none, who make the most fanatical adherents.

People Power

After the collective orgy of emotion, the collective hangover. Journalists search among mounds of wilting flowers for something new to say and, even as they search, new flowers arrive, as if the People were loth to let their frenzy go. The People! People Power! As he deftly manipulates the situation for his own political purposes, Mr Blair knows only too well the force of those resonant catchwords.

Like a garish, fairground inflatable, the monster of "People Power" emerged from among the million mourners of London — a strange kind of mourners, to be sure, with their cameras, sloppy clothes and air of carnival! This was a new, feeble kind of mob, with a large proportion of youngish women in it, sentimental, fashion-crazed, modelling themselves on "soap" characters, ignorant, but not in the ordinary sense, for their heads are stuffed with received opinions and false televisionary information.

If these unfortunates are the People, what kind of power can the People have? What will they do when the real world invades their world of illusion, when something really serious hits them, not in the imagined lives of the famous but in their own lives? Where they will hide? There will be no more refuge within the television screen.

A Holy Rage

Nerdley University is a pioneer in the transformation of Academia from a stuffy, port-stained morass peopled by snuff-taking, wing-collared elitist has-beens into a brand new, gleaming arena for democratic intellectual endeavour. It was the first university in this country to appoint visiting professors in non-smoking studies, lager lout studies, fat cat studies, alcopop studies and other vital contemporary disciplines.

It has just appointed Britain's first visiting professor in road rage studies. He is Royston Cylinder, a member of the Supreme Army Council of J. Bonington Jagworth's Motorists' Liberation Front and therefore close to the latest research on this subject. He is a Marxist fundamentalist. Although he drives a Boggs Super Yobbo, he wears bicycle clips and steel-rimmed NHS spectacles of traditional design and carries a complete set of Stalin's works in the glove compartment. His sallow, fanatical face is deeply grooved with lines of Hegelian dialectic.

He will find plenty of like-minded academics at Nerdley. But his new job has not gone down so well with the MLF. "Don't go in for books and that sort of stuff myself," Jagworth said at a meeting in their luxurious inspection-pit H.Q. "somewhere near Staines". He is fond of recalling how he was sent down from Oxford after driving a "clapped out old banger" into the Bodleian Library.

"Well, Cylinder can do as he pleases. What d'you think, padre? You're the brainy one." The Rev John Goodwheel, chaplain-general to the MLF, known to millions as the "Apostle of the Motorways", thoughtfully fingered the gold pectoral spanner which hangs from his neck. "Road rage — yes, a natural impatience with the typical slow, cautious driver — is beginning to concern our more forward-looking automobilistic theologians more and more," he murmured.

"We have always held that road rage is not merely justified but at its highest can be a form of prayer, an expression of the Holy in a very real sense. But now some of us are coming to believe that all vehicles are equal; that the right attitude is a caring one. We must feel compassion for the slow cautious driver even as we crowd him into the ditch."

"Oh, come off it, padre!" Jagworth growled, while Cylinder began bawling that road rage was essentially a cry for help from the motoring victims of institutionalised oppression in the crisis of late 20th century automobilism.

Performance Art

The council of the Royal Academy has formally rebuked Norman Rosenthal, its exhibitions secretary who organised the "Sensation" exhibition, with its infamous portrait of Myra Hindley. But the rebuke was not for that but for insulting an octogenenarian painter, John Ward, by suggesting that he was not much of an artist. However the council refused to sack Mr Rosenthal but passed a vote of confidence in him instead. Mr Ward himself has now resigned.

This is all very disappointing. I had been hoping for a masterpiece of performance art, in which, after Mr Rosenthal had been formally sacked, Mr Ward would be given the chance, if he wished, to punch him formally on the nose before an invited audience, including the two distinguished performance artists who threw eggs and paint at Myra Hindley's portrait when the exhibition opened.

Mr Rosenthal would then have been pushed formally through the Academy doors and down the steps into the courtyard, while some of the more spectacularly destructible items of rubbish in his exhibition — tanks

of formaldehyde and so forth — were flung after him and the decent
Academy cleaners waved their mops and brushes in triumph.

"A compelling and committed statement for our time... tautly organised with a dynamically and financially firm control of multilinear form...
of the dilemma of the pop exhibition secretary in our fragmented world
of existential flux..." (276 art critics)

Health

Hundreds of thousands of medical research scientists are working on the
dangers of passive smoking, red meat eating, sunbathing, accordion playing and numberless threats to health.

But only Dr Ron Hardware's pioneering team at Nerdley University
is gathering all these threats together in a "grand unified field theory" of
public health.

In a series of laboratory experiments, a young fit man and a 75 year
old man suffering from emphysema, Ménière's disease, pemphigus and
other ailments were confined in separate cardboard boxes while both ate
red meat.

Tobacco smoke in dense concentration was pumped only into the old
man's box. After 30 minutes he showed symptoms of severe strain
whereas the young man was unaffected.

"It's early days yet," Dr Hardware says. "But a link between red
meat eating, passive smoking and heart disease is strongly indicated.
Now we hope to do research on other health hazards in combination —
for example, passive smoking, red meat eating, racism, fox hunting and
so on.

"In our democracy the public has a right to know the results of the
latest scientific research. The media have a duty to publicise it at length
in articles which have to be 'sensational' and give us scientists prominent mention if they to be taken seriously at all.

"Our new work is going to need a lot more public relations staff,
laboratory staff and equipment. It is going to cost a lot more money. A
crash programme of research looking as far ahead as the year 2050, funded
by a large government grant, perhaps from the lottery...."

Discuss

A Hollywood film based on Heinrich Harrer's book *Seven Years in Tibet*
tells how this Austrian mountaineer and explorer, interned in India at the

beginning of the Second World War, escaped with a companion and after two years reached Lhasa.

There he not only fell in love with Tibetan ways, but also became tutor to the young Dalai Lama, and a general favourite. A film of this exciting story would seem to have everything going for it. It will appeal both to devotees of fashionable Buddhism and to those who are rightly angry at the Chinese conquest of Tibet and the cruel destruction of its people and their ancient order.

However, some kind, public-spirited person suddenly revealed that Harrer, now 85, had been a member of the Nazi party before the war and skiing instructor to the SS.

All hell immediately broke loose. There are those for whom having once been a member of the Nazi party stamps a man as wholly and irredeemably evil. In their eyes, it may even outweigh the evil of Chinese crimes in Tibet.

But others may reflect that in this world, nothing is all of a piece: not even the Nazi party. Mightn't a man have been a member of the Nazi party and still, however deluded, an honourable and decent man? And here is another awkward, tangential question. Had they been victorious, wouldn't the Nazis, with their ecological and mystical tendencies, have saved Tibet? Discuss.

Arts and Crafts

Mountwarlock in Leicestershire, the ancient seat of Lord Mountwarlock, offers visitors a "safari park" of fabulous monsters, a "Dark Age Banquet Hall of Dread" with horribly realistic features, "Circe's Boutique", the "Shirt of Nessus" Men's Shop and many other unusual attractions. It is also open all the year round, and is thought to be the only "stately home" where the number of visitors who leave it is often smaller than the number who enter.

Large parts of the tenebrous domains, heathland and forest, are closed to the public, an affront to the Ramblers Association. When Jim Yagoda, chief developmental and policy co-ordinator of the Stretchford Branch, dispatched a 20 strong commando of elite "footpath fighters" to assert "the right to roam" there, he gave them a stirring pep talk, exhorting them to strike at this bastion of medieval superstition, feudal oppression and obsolete rights of private property "with pitiless rigour" and establish the People's Will "for a thousand years".

Striking boldly into the ghoul-haunted woodland, the commandos were soon lost in a confusion of forking, indeed shifting, paths. They did not realize either, that they were being watched from behind the trees by Phantomsby, the Earl's factotum, one of the few practising werewolves remaining in the Midlands. Although the moon was past the full and a square meal out of the question, Phantomsby thought that by growling and occasionally howling in a blood-curdling way he could "give them something to think about" and even send them running in panic to the outer world.

But as they stood about fiddling with maps disordered by a sudden supernatural gale from nowhere, a gorgon which had escaped from the "safari park" appeared in their way and turned them all to stone in an instant. Later on, Phantomsby offered this unusual group of statuary to Ghoulman, who runs the Garden Centre of Terror. But he rejected it as likely to frighten off prospective customers.

"What about the Tate Gallery?" Phantomsby said. "Wouldn't they like to have it? Haven't you got a cousin there, that Mr Serota or something?"

"Nah", Ghoulman said with a dismissive gesture, "They're representational, see? Don't express the spirit of the age. He wouldn't touch 'em not if he lived a million years, as he probably will."

Treat In Store

This year, the GPI Television Network's Christmas programmes will have even wider appeal than usual. According to a handout, the popular Christmas Day sex quiz *Know what I mean?*, presented by Dave Gradbag, will have a "predominantly gay and lesbian flavour" and will be a "real treat for all the family".

The Royal element, traditional at Christmas, is represented by an illustrated talk on the restoration of Windsor Castle, with the republican architect, militant atheist and sauce chef Jonathan Gloves denouncing royal waste and ostentation, and calling for the castle to be converted into a People's republican theme park with St George's Chapel as a museum of humanism.

On the cosier, domestic side, *Freedom Fighters*, a documentary about a typical IRA family, offers unusual insight into the intimate lives of these controversial, widely misunderstood people, with glimpses of home bomb-maker and mother-of-seven Rita MacSeedy, of bluff, lovable Brigadier Sean MacGuffog, with his quirky tales of operations against the Brits in south Armagh, and many other appealing characters.

The traditional Christmas sing-song of workers' ballads from the Rentacrowd folksong factory (founded by the late Ewan MacColl) has been dropped this year as "too elitist". Instead there will be a three-hour programme of multi-racial techno rap introduced by Jim Ogbufe and Noel Dreadberg.

"We want to get right away from the moribund image that Christmas has had so long and make it relevant, sexy and above all youth-orientated, so as to interact more effectively with the customers," says the GPI chairman, Sir Godfrey Fobster.

"Inevitably there will be groans from a vociferous minority of Tory has-beens, reactionary blimps, 'Disgusted of Cheltenham', prissy chapel-goers and so on. But the angrier they are, the more we at GPI will enjoy our People's Yuletide."

Challenge

Bone Eldritch Mackenzie, the mammoth public relations group which became famous 30 years ago for its promotion of National Tarantula Week, has pulled off a sensational coup. It has got the Saddam Hussein account for an undisclosed sum thought to run into billions. Will it succeed in making him one of the most popular personalities in the world? "It is the kind of challenge we enjoy," says a spokesman.

"B.E.M." has never had a failure yet. There are all kinds of possibilities. One is a gigantic rock festival near Baghdad, coinciding with a reopening of the Hanging Gardens of Babylon. Or Saddam may bid for the moral leadership of the world by declaring Iraq the first country to impose the death penalty for smoking.

Veiled

In Bradford, which has a Muslim population of 70,000, a Muslim woman was ordered off a bus because she refused to lift her veil so that the driver could check her face against the photograph in her travel pass. The bus was held up for 20 minutes. She complained to the bus company and asked the driver to apologise.

Although the Stretchford Conurbation has a much smaller number of Muslims, such incidents are quite common there. Many middle-aged and elderly women belonging to the "ethnic majority" have taken to wearing veils when they travel on buses. Some believe it gives them "an air of mystery", others that it spares other people the shock of seeing their faces. Others believe it "keeps out the dust".

But most wear veils because it gives them a chance of refusing to show their faces to the driver for checking against their passes. This

means they can hold up the bus for long periods — a mere 20 minutes is
thought derisory — while ferocious arguments develop among the other
passengers, preferably leading to blows and an order from the driver:
"Everybody off! I don't care who you are! I said, everybody off!"
"It sort of cheers me up when skies are dull and grey" says Mrs Eileen
Pedestal, a 60 year old widow who wears four veils on bus journeys,
readily removing three on request but refusing to remove the fourth. "It
usually causes a terrible row and holds people up for hours," she says,
"But deep down I think they enjoy it. It's what they call a consciousness-
raising experience."

Read On

Books for younger kids this Christmas (writes Pippa Banshee) are breaking new ground. Out go nauseous tales about cute talking animals, "nice"
white middle-class English families, twee countryside adventures. Into
the bin, thank goodness, thud the likes of A.A. Milne, Lewis Carroll and
Beatrix Potter (who she?).
    Today's three to six year olds demand realism above all. They insist
on a hopeful, caring attitude, emotional literacy and wholehearted commitment to New Britain. Picture books about Tony Blair, Jack Straw,
Mike Meacher and, above all, Peter Mandelson, a tremendous favourite
with the kids, are in great demand. I particularly liked Eve Nogg's *Molly's
Millennium* (Viper & Bugloss, £9.99) about the adventures of a typical
four-year-old New Labour supporter in search of Peter's Magic Dome.
    Jim the Excluded by Tom Harbrace (V&P, £7.99) is a thrilling story
about a typical six-year-old deprived "inner-city" youngster with four
single parents, one white, one black, one Asian and one Australian aboriginal, all bisexual. Jim Leroy Anand Gugatjira Smith is excluded when
he truants from his south London school. He becomes in turn a drug
dealer with a big revolver, a social worker dealing with paedophiles, and
a bent detective, and finally finds fulfilment as a billionaire Left-wing
rock club proprietor.
    Kids today demand total honesty in sexual matters. Joan Grough's
marvellous *Condom Fairies* uses a fairyland background not to propa-
gate harmful escapist fantasies, but to drive home the lessons of safe sex
— with forceful five-year-old hero Pattie making sure that everybody in
her village learns and practises it. (Toadstone Press, £25.99, with introduction by Heinz Kiosk and Melisande Fischbein).

A Bit of Sense

Mrs Elvira Mutcliffe, who runs a well-respected coven near Sowerby Bridge in the West Riding, is put out by the undue publicity given to the fairies by a current exhibition at the Royal Academy.

"As a serious witch," she says, "I take little or no cognisance of these tiresome little beings with their silly diaphanous wings and simpering ways."

"There have been occasions when bands of them have tried to 'muscle in' on our coven meetings. They seem to know that these are normally held on the first Tuesday afternoon of the month, when we have afternoon tea, scones and cakes within the magic pentacle in my lounge before invoking the Great Black Goat of Mytholmroyd.

"His visits are all too rare and he is much less likely to manifest if these fairies are hanging about to put him off his infernal stroke. Fortunately we have a useful deterrent in Councillor Albert Gogden, our Chief Warlock and Keeper of the Trilby Hat of Invisibility.

"Albert has his faults. He is inclined to be greedy and more than once I have had to rap him sharply over the knuckles with the cake slice to stop him reaching over and grabbing my home-made Eccles cakes and dainty jam sponges from Elaine, my second-in-command, who is in overall charge of the comestibles.

"But if there are fairies about, he has only to raise his hand to send them shimmering off in double-quick time to wherever they come from. Good riddance to bad rubbish!"

Noel

Christmas at Bog Lane Primary School at Nerdley has always been ecumenical and multi-cultural. This year with Dr Spaceley-Trellis, the dynamic, go-ahead bishop of the newly renamed diocese of Bevindon and Stretchford, taking an active part, it will be more ecumenical and multicultural than ever.

As well as some of the less elitist characters in the Nativity story, the Christmas crib will include figures of heroes and benefactors of humanity from Karl Marx to Nelson Mandela. As Dr Trellis says, this is "a proof of commitment to the core values of progressive religion in a very real sense, in a form which all school kids can readily understand."

In the multi-faith Nativity play, scripted by the Bishop's partner, the Rev Mantissa Shout, the former pioneering deaconess and militant feminist, all faiths will be represented on an equal footing. Fortunately, there is plenty of acting talent among the pupils, three-quarters of whom are non-white, and the staff, whose versatile head, Dr Ron Ogbufe, at one time worked in the Institute of Necromancy in Bungrafts (formerly New Harrogate) in Gombola, under President Ngrafta himself.

Myths of the Australian Aboriginals, tribal tales of the Amazonian rainforest and other people once little regarded but now greatly admired, will all have a place. There will be a strong feminist element. Mantissa has promised to perform her ritual dance of praise to the Great Green Earth Mother, accompanied by gifted pupils on the Papuan nose-flute and the Tasmanian linoleum harp. There will be readings from the Koran, Buddhist hymns, and controversial Tantric ceremonies.

There are several Aztec pupils at the school, including Sheryl Huitzilopochtli, five-year-old daughter of the Atzec community leader Royston Huitzilopochtli (formerly South Shields-born 41st-year sociology student Royston Nobes). His demand that the Nativity play shall include traditional Aztec ceremonies, particularly human sacrifice, is causing problems.

The police have regretfully warned the school that human sacrifice is still illegal in Britain. Cllr Don Binliner, the Labour chairman of the Nerdley Education Authority, has denounced this as "an unacceptable relic of outmoded racism... the Atzec community is a force for multicultural progress and an example to the rest of the country. Nerdley should be proud of it".

Thought

In a speech to the African Congress in Mafeking, which won him a great ovation and the bonus of a big hug from his ex-wife Winnie, Nelson Mandela is reported to have said that the "next century would belong to Africa". I sometimes feel rather gloomy about the future of the world myself. But I have never thought of anything quite like that.

What the Papers Say

In a thoughtful leader, *The Feudal Times* and *Reactionary Herald* surveys the course of the Old Year and the prospects for the New: "A good many of our readers, for obvious reasons, cannot sit in the House of Commons or vote in parliamentary elections. Yet many, in the course of managing their estates and attending to their own concerns, take a keen interest in parliamentary affairs.

"They will be aware, therefore, that the overthrow of the so-called 'Conservative' faction and the accession to power with a large majority of the so-called 'Labour' faction will make little difference to those tendencies which for many years have set our country on such a disastrous course.

"The new dispensation merely strengthens and accelerates those baleful tendencies. It brings a new and yet uglier, because more confident, stridency to the voice of an odious gang of foaming radicals, sophistical levellers, fashionable perverts and degenerate mountebanks. It seeks to give further credence to the deadly myth of 'multiculturalism'. It toadies to the commercial interest and elevates the vulgar bagman, the huckster and the fairground barker to the highest councils of the Realm.

"The very nicknames by which the principal ministers of the new government choose to be known to the public — 'Tony', 'Mo' and so forth — can only indicate their low-mindedness and their wish to pander to the low-bred and trivial-minded.

"Instead of denouncing the onrush of vile, barbarous and obscene entertainment, now ceaselessly disseminated throughout the country by novel electro-galvanic devices to the wellnigh universal corruption of hearts and minds, they go out of their way — like their predecessors, alas! — to flatter and honour its oafish, debauched and insanitary exponents, and even welcome them to their official receptions.

"Instead of enacting serious measures to meet the threats of crime and disorder at home and malign conspiracies abroad, they seek to govern by the continual extrusion of gaseous moralistic verbiage. They employ prodigious new methods of lying and disinformation whose adepts are so confident of the stupidity of their victims that they will openly and shamelessly avow what they are doing, and — a thing hitherto unheard of — are actually commended for it!

"A significant event of the past year was the sad death, in a motoring accident, of the eccentric Princess of Wales, much loved by the people, which set off an astounding outbreak of lachrymose frenzy, all the more alarming and even sinister for being instantly seized on and manipulated by official soul-doctors and soothsayers for the further deception and entrapment of the multitude

"If there be hope, it lies in signs of rebellion against a debased metropolis by stalwart English people in the remaining rural areas, ostensibly in defence of foxhunting, but really, we believe, in defence of everything we mean by the English nation.

"Can the spirit of these admirable people defeat the evil tendencies which gathered so much force in the Old Year and will gather even more force in the New, when all manner of detestable projects are to be brought forward: the abolition of the hereditary principle in the House of Lords, our ultimate safeguard against darkness and chaos; the disintegration of the Realm itself and its piecemeal surrender to the vain and fraudulent entity called 'Europe'?

"We confess to nursing a last, wan hope: no less than a grand alliance against these evils between English countrymen and the still decent and honest, though dispossessed, English working men of the industrial districts. If that should prove a mere chimera, what hope remains?"

Mystery

During excavations in the crypt of All Saints Church at Nerdley, the head of the Archaeology Department at Nerdley University, Dr John Goodmound, discovered an old manuscript, dust-covered but surprisingly well preserved, which may revolutionise all our accepted ideas about the medieval Mystery Plays.

According to Dr Norman Goodlit, head of the English Faculty at Nerdley, the Nerdley Mystery Play, unlike others, does not accuse the Jews of being guilty of Christ's death. On the contrary. In a long speech an unidentified Archangel commends the Jews, in so many words, for "their outstandingly helpful attitude in what must have been a testing and difficult time for them and all those concerned in this unusual series of events". He also commends Pilate and the Roman authorities for their "sympathetic handling of very complex issues".

In another key passage, the Disciples, who include equal numbers of men and women, condemn "sexism" and "racism" and call for co-ordinated action to enforce "race and sex equality" throughout the Roman Empire, with appropriate boards and liaison committees in each province, particularly in those, such as Cappadocia, which have "large and varied ethnic minorities".

In a long speech during Christ's entry into Jerusalem, the Disciple Peter condemns smoking and demands a ban on this "wicked and unhygienic habit" in all taverns throughout the city. In a controversial passage, another Disciple, Thomas, calls for a boycott of South African goods, particularly grapefruit.

"Citrus fruits were, of course, an important part of the Judaean economy," says Dr Goodlit. "But," he admits, "there are some difficulties about the precise dating of the manuscript. We cannot entirely rule out a prophetic element, however much this goes against the grain of modern scholarship. We have to consider all possibilities on their merits."

The Vicar of All Saints, the Rev John Variables, hopes to put on a first performance of the play as part of the Nerdley Arts Festival this summer. "Marylou Ogreburg and her People's Bread and Marmite Multiracial Dance Theatre Group would be ideal for it," he said. "If we could only get Vaclav's Dvorak's Mime Group to come over from the Czech Republic as well, our cup of joy would be pressed down and running over," he added with an infectious laugh which had bystanders running for cover.

Dr Spaceley-Trellis, the go-ahead Bishop of Bevindon and Stretchford, and Chairman of Football Managers for a Multi-Faith Millennium, is also keen. In his long-term plans he is thinking of a place for the Nerdley Mystery Play as "a key religious element in the Millennium Dome in a very real sense".

A Sad Business

Veteran readers of this column (a dwindling band, as Narcolept, our boring expert, never fails to say) may wonder, now that the "problem of football hooliganism" has hundreds of experts working on it night and day, together with task forces and advisory boards, whatever became of the pioneering hooligans of the Stretchford Conurbation?

By the early 1970s these fans of rival teams, Stretchford United and Nerdley Wanderers, had transformed hooliganism from mere brutish violence into an art. The actual matches they attended were of minor interest. Only Albert Rasp, Stretchford's legendary goal-conceding goalkeeper, a giant of ineptitude among his inept team-mates, was outstanding.

What counted, and was reported in millions of empurpled words by colourfully illiterate sports writers, was the hooliganism itself. How could it be otherwise, when a match that started with a commonplace exchange of missiles — toilet rolls and massive lumps of solidified risotto, progressing to wardrobes and rusting car bodies — might end with the invasion of the pitch, hand-to-hand fighting, the stands on fire and the whole of Stretchford's Effluent Road ground or Nerdley's Anthrax Park under six feet of water?

By the mid-1970s the fans were using "Roman army-type" ballistas to hurl grand pianos and pantechnicons loaded with poisoned potato crisps for immense distances. What went wrong? Why did this "phenomenal explosion of creative energy", as Dr Heinz Kiosk calls it in his classic study *Aspects of Football Hooliganism in a West Midland City* (1978) falter and die?

Like so many things beautiful, monstrous or both together, football hooliganism as an art seems to have been one more victim of the ravening, yet well-meaning, spirit of democracy. Some of its ablest practitioners, true artists in their day, developed what they nauseatingly called a "social conscience". Some fell for the new, fashionable talk of football as "a bridge between the nations" or "an ambassador for Britain".

Some even stooped to working for the Football Association as special advisers on hooliganism. But the knell of this traditional pastime of Old England sounded when Dr E. W. T. Spaceley-Trellis, the go-ahead Bishop of Bevindon, announced that hooliganism must no longer be the preserve of a privileged elitist few; it was the birthright of all. Soon all that remained was the dull, stereotyped, unimaginative hooliganism of our day.

Only last week a reunion of sadly wizened hooligans, veterans of the old days, took place at the Effluent Road ground, now derelict. It was a melancholy occasion. When Jack Krakatoa, winner of the Desmond Fobster challenge cup for the Best Feat of Individual Hooliganism six years running, feebly tried to hurl part of a deckchair a few yards he immediately doubled up and fell to the ground, groaning and cursing his arthritis.

In the fading light of the winter afternoon the ghost of Albert Rasp rose gibbering and squeaking from the waterlogged ground, and the hooligans fled. Had they realised that the site has been earmarked by Stretchford Sports Council, lottery funds permitting, for a £25 million Centre of Football Excellence, they would have died of shame.

Residential

Mr Quentin Goth-Jones, director of Stretchford Arts, who belongs to one of the most influential families in the conurbation, claims it has appointed more artists-in-residence than any other local authority. He believes they are "doing a vital job for Britain as the creative arts centre of the world by building bridges between the arts and the community and forging links between the community and the arts world". There are artists-in-residence in most factories, hospitals, police stations, employment agencies and supermarkets. It is estimated that there are at least 60 in the Nadirco Consumerama in Soup Hales alone, working under a principal artist-in-residence, Clare Goth-Jones, who sees their work as "a bid to build vital links between the arts and the community". One of them, Monica Goth-Jones, who took a degree in supermarket performance art at Gnomesall Heath University, is working in the medium of staging collisions between old age pensioners' loaded trolleys by shining powerful lights in their eyes. Julian Goth-Jones, who studied rubbish sculpture under the great Jon Ghasbin and has had a one-man show at Lampton-on-Hoke Council Refuse Disposal Department's Unit One Gallery, is working on timed "mini-ava-lanches" of stacked pet food tins, while his cousin and live-in girlfriend, Paula Goth-Jones, photographs them with a filmless camera, "producing blank images of astonishing power".

As well as visual artists, there are several rap-composers in-residence and a self-styled Australian aboriginal linoleum harpist-in-residence, Gus Goth-Jones, who works at the alternative gas meter readers' training school at Nerdbridge. Most people agree that all these artists-in-resi-dence are "doing a wonderful job promoting awareness of the links be-tween the arts and the community".

But a few are doubtful. "There are far too many of them," says Mrs Karen Djugashvili, a Nerdley pensioner. "You never know where they've been. Only the other morning I opened the door of my fridge and two of them popped out, asked the way to the nearest arts centre and walked off, cool as you please. I know they're doing their best for Britain, like it says, forging bridges between the creative arts and the community world. But I can't help asking, whatever next?"

Memories

As everybody knows, what Stretchford thinks today, England will think tomorrow. Today, hundreds of women in the conurbation are claiming, often in lurid detail, to have had sexual intercourse with Mr Clinton during his triumphal visit to this country in furtherance of the "peace process" in Ulster ("two years ago, was it? It seems like yesterday").

Experts think many of these women, some of whom are well over 70, may be former members of the militant Our Jack Kennedy Fan Club, now disbanded, and that they may have been expelled for failing to claim to have had sexual intercourse with Kennedy himself.

"Bill Clinton caught my eye when he drove through Stretchford to open the new sex advice clinic in St Oick's Road," recalls Mrs Karen MacMarrow, 72, of Nerdley. "Acting on his instructions, an aide or source or something — I don't know which, my head was in such a whirl — took me to the clinic, along with a lot of other women, in a transit van complete with motorcycle outriders and all.

"After we had had sexual intercourse, each of us was given a five-dollar bill and a jumbo-size packet of coffee 'n' blueberry flavour pop tarts. But I never ate mine.

"I still keep them, intact if a bit stale, in a glass case, to remind me of a true gentleman and lover of women whom Fate has called upon to be president of the greatest nation on earth," she went on, apparently reading the words off the ceiling. "The annoying thing is that I could have sold my impressions of Bill to a tabloid and perhaps had them syndicated throughout the world and been rich beyond the dreams of Croesus. Is it too late?"

Hero

He has gone, the last of the great English patriots, the last English tragic hero. At a time when patriotism, like heroism, is unfashionable in England, even grudging obituaries of Enoch Powell commended his love of country and his commitment to principle. But even the most favourable insisted that he was plain wrong about one thing: immigration.

But was he wrong? Certainly the inter-racial bloodletting he feared — but not, as is falsely said, prophesied and even incited — has not yet come about. But was he wrong to believe that mass immigration would be one of the factors — perhaps the most important factor of all — that would transform England into a country no longer recognisable as the country it had been?

As an English patriot, he opposed all threats to English identity: as well as immigration: he opposed England's absorption into the bogus entity called "Europe"; he opposed the dwindling of England into an American satellite; and, had he kept his health and strength, he would have opposed the creeping totalitarianism of the Blairite state.

No "racist", he saw how the immigrants, however innocent in themselves, would be used as an instrument by those who wanted to change England for ever. "Immigration is the fulcrum," he told me at a meeting 30 years ago, intoning the word in that strange, intense, unforgettable West Midlands accent of his. "It is the fulcrum by which England is to be overturned."

And from outside the hall, as he spoke, came the sound of a regimented mob of hate-crazed idealist stormtroopers for One World and the Brotherhood of Man, baying in rhythmic slogans for his patriot blood.

Well, they have won. If there really was a conspiracy, it has exceeded the hopes of any imaginable conspirators. A whole great industry, supported by all the apparatus of the state, has grown up to persuade us that

England, part-colonised, has turned into a multi-racial society; and that this is not merely an established fact, but an unquestionably good thing for everybody concerned.

It has been made virtually illegal to discuss the matter seriously and honestly. A paralysing neurotic disorder has seized on us, making us unable to speak easily, even in private, for fear of being thought "racist". Yet in the only sense in which Powell was "racist" — he actually thought there were recognisable differences between races! — almost everybody was a "racist" before Hitler gave it a bad name, and most people are "racist" still. How can we live in this world without a certain prejudice in favour of ourselves?

A tragic hero? Had Powell been less scrupulous, less deeply in love with English history, its ancient, ordered continuity, he might have seized that moment 30 years ago when he was at once the most acclaimed and the most execrated man in England. He might have become leader of the Conservative Party and in due course prime minister, with greater popular support than any in our history.

Perhaps fancifully, I imagine this eccentric, noble-hearted man putting that tremendous vision aside, not through weakness but through virtue, determined not to risk bringing harm to his country through disruptive action even in a good cause. That is why he is a tragic hero, and will become a legend.

Visit

One of the less publicised events of Mr Clinton's African tour was his visit to Gombola (formerly Gomboland) and his meeting with President Ngrafta, thought to be the only head of state in the world who, as well as holding a first-class degree from the London School of Economics, is a practising witch-doctor (Grade I), specialising in the production of thought forms.

Addressing a delirious crowd of millions in the capital Bungrafta (formerly New Harrogate), with Dr Ngrafta beside him, smiling and making traditional Gombolan gestures with his ceremonial flywhisk, Mr Clinton spoke of the historic links, dating from the very dawn of history, between Gombola and the United States of America:

"It is for us now to forge a new forging of old and new and carry forward all that is best in our two cultures, both age-old wisdom and advanced technology, into the global order that beckons humanity ever onward from the past and present to the future and vice versa."

Perhaps noticing that miscellaneous thought forms, as well as two-headed giants, serpent spirits and forest demons, were well represented in the crowd, he brought his speech to a rather uncertain end.

Meanwhile Dr Ngrafta, who at the beginning of the speech had worn a formal frock coat and top hat, used his magical arts to switch bewilderingly between flowing, many-coloured Gombolan robes, the uniform of a Roman centurion, Elizabethan court dress and a Croydon car-dealer's blazer and "cavalry twill" trousers. On and off, for good measure, he made himself invisible.

Later Mr Clinton "went on walkabout" with his host through the streets of Bungrafta, which, as he did not fail to remark, is "a fascinating mixture of old and new".

Towering white concrete-and-glass skyscrapers and ultra-modern hotels with swimming pools and lifts in every room loom over picturesque alleys of mud huts (there are also some mud skyscrapers).

Here the vibrant, colourful life of Old Gombola, with its huge-bosomed market women ("aunties"), its cakefruit sellers, wooden tuning fork makers, luminous sponge jugglers, musicians playing hungs (a kind of very loud xylopohone), deaf-aid adjusters, bookmakers' runners, dealers in magic love philtres and enormous aphrodisiac toenails, and hundreds of other agreeably pointless traders and craftsmen, is still unchanged from time immemorial.

As the two statesmen walked among the high-spirited but good-natured crowd, cordially discussing world peace and trade relations, Ngrafta could not resist displaying his powers further.

In an instant he altered the weather from blazing sunshine to a monsoon deluge and back again. He made subtle adjustments to streets and buildings. At one point the whole city seemed to dwindle and vanish down a black hole constructed on the very latest astrophysical principles.

As a final treat, he projected a thought form of Mr Clinton himself dictating to a woman secretary in the Oval Office, then stood back beaming with professional pride, defying anybody to distinguish between the phantom president and the "real" one.

Musical Menace

A report by Norman Lebrecht about a group of pianists in Stockholm who performed the complete symphonies of Mahler in piano version in a single day has dismayed members of the old Stretchford Municipal Symphony Orchestra. Most of them are now retired and doing their best to forget the very name of Mahler.

When the orchestra was forcibly disbanded by the council in 1987 as part of a "cultural redeployment programme" and replaced by a municipal "centre for rock music excellence", its veteran conductor, the Mahler-crazed Sir Jim Gastropodi, returned to his native Poggibonsi in Tuscany, where he spends most of his time searching in attics, with varying success, for manuscripts of hitherto undiscovered Mahler symphonies.

So far he claims to have found "about 25" fully orchestrated scores and half a dozen mere sketches, with typical parts for tubular bells, muted horns and massed contrabassoons. Musicologists are, of course, divided over the order and number of Mahler's symphonies. Some believe he wrote only one symphony, if that; others that the number is infinite.

Safe from Mahler at last, as they thought, in their cosy homes in leafy Stretchford suburbs, Sir Jim's "lads and lasses" are devoted to various unmusical hobbies, from cheese label collecting to home blastfurnace construction. So the news from Stockholm affected them in different ways. Miss Hilda Craggs, whose stringless harp called for superlative musicianship in the old days, gave a silent scream and began convulsively twanging her knitting needles.

But Ron Spheroyd, the 25-stone West Riding-born principal bass tuba and former Supreme High Archimandrite of the Basilica of the Stretchford branch of the Musicians' Union (no humble Father of the Chapel he), rose majestically from his armchair and seemed to swell to twice his ordinary size. Then, seizing his tuba from the corner and dusting it off, he blew the prodigious B flat, which to musicians everywhere signifies "All out!" — and heroically expired.

Guilty Men

Voice for Choice, a parliamentary group campaigning for the liberalisation of the abortion laws, believes doctors should be required to declare whether or not they support abortion. They have too much freedom, says the group's chairman, Baroness Gould of Potternewton, to use moral rather than medical judgments. Those who oppose abortion should be named in a register.

Dr Llewelyn Goth-Jones, the condom-crazed, fluoride-stuffed director of community medicine for the Stretchford Conurbation, thinks this does not go nearly far enough. "The names of these guilty men should be published in the press and on posters as widely as possible. The public must be protected from so-called doctors — they are simply quacks and charlatans — who think there is any place in modern medical practice for reactionary, superstitious, so-called 'moral' judgments.

"They should be exposed as the dangerous fanatics they are. After a formal warning and a chance to repent by declaring their readiness to carry out abortions on demand, they should be hauled before the General Medical Council and struck off for infamous conduct, preferably in a public ceremony. If they can't be trusted with abortions, they can't be trusted with any other medical treatment."

Constant

Thinking of the scare about the "Millennium bug", which is supposed to send computers crazy on the last day of the century, I went to see our columnar computer, "Ughtred St John Mainwaring" (no vulgar "Bert" or "Jim" for us).

I found it humming quietly to itself in its finely wrought rosewood cabinet, while Mr Grylls, the retired clergyman who looks after this venerable machine, sat dozing beside it, a volume of Burton's *Anatomy of Melancholy* slipping off his knees.

"Bug, sir?" He winced slightly. "There'll be no trouble of that kind with him," (he always refers to his august charge in this respectful way). "He still keeps to the time of Queen Anne, when he was born, and thanks to what is technically called 'eternal' programming, he will ignore a mere change of century."

"I am glad to hear it, Grylls. See he has everything he needs for keeping time at bay." Mr Grylls nodded. He poured a decanter of old port into the machine, which at once responded with a strange, deep, almost purring sound that seemed to be on the very verge of articulacy. At the same time it extruded the following verbal material: "Thank 'ee kindly, Parson Grylls".

In the Bunker

J. Bonington Jagworth, Supreme Leader of the Motorists' Liberation Front, called a meeting of his staff in their inspection-pit bunker "somewhere near Staines" to affirm their "resolute support" for the Birmingham Northern Relief Road. If it is built, this will be the first toll motorway in England, a triumph for the motorists' cause and a disaster for their enemies.

"I hear those miserable environmental creeps are opposing it in the courts," Jagworth bellowed. "Even worse, those filthy, snivelling little eco-creatures have already started digging tunnels and climbing trees all over the place. The law is far too soft on that scum.

"Padre, why don't you preach the moral motoring argument against them? Can't you pronounce a, what d'you call it, anathema? Blast them off the face of the Earth? Go on, it's all yours."

The Rev. John Goodwheel, chaplain-general to the MLF, known to millions as "the Apostle of the Motorways", smiled gently as he touched his pectoral spanner with pious, oil-stained fingers. "No, no," he murmured. "Today we motoring priests seek to affirm our motoring ideals not by aggressive proselytism but by dialogue, understanding and compassion. Above all, we avoid confrontation and judgmental attitudes."

Quietly he explained his plan to take his mobile romanesque cathedral on a "mission tour" of key sites on the projected motorway route and preach the automobilistic gospel to the unconverted.

But Jagworth, growing more and more impatient, soon lost his temper altogether, angrily sloshing BGA and brake fluid alternately into his silver presentation hubcap at a prodigious rate, while Royston Cylinder, the crypto-Marxist, atheist chief-of-staff, sneered even more horribly than usual at his old opponent.

"Religious motorists are merely sprinkling holy water on the historic speed-limit-enforcing oppressors," he yelled. The meeting broke up when Jagworth, seeking relief from this eternal dispute, rushed to the wheel of his Boggs Super-Yobbo and was soon roaring away at 120 mph in the general direction of Birmingham.

Give us the Facts

Another forthcoming BBC enterprise is a documentary about Lord Kitchener and his crimes, mitigated, perhaps, by his alleged homosexual tendencies. But will the programme deal with the real facts about this British war hero? Did he really perish when his ship was mined off Orkney on his mission to Russia in 1916?

Or did he, as some historians believe, survive to land in Russia and eventually emerge as Stalin, who bore such a convenient facial resemblance to him? Some historians also believe that Stalin-Kitchener did not die in 1953, but escaped from his enemies in the Kremlin and made his way to America. There, minus his moustache and with a partial reversion to his original surname, he eventually emerged as Kissinger and so went on playing a mysteriously important part in world affairs.

This theory is disputed by other historians, who believe it conflicts with accepted laws of space and time. There is one sure way of testing it. Kitchener is known to have been an extreme aelurophobe. The mere presence of a cat in a neighbouring room was enough to reduce this otherwise brave man to uncontrolled trembling. Is anything known on this score about Stalin or Kissinger?

On the Ohm Farm

"Talk about genetically modified foods! Whoy, dang me purple! They Yanks in Monsanto Corporation do be talkin' big now, but us'n at Ohm Farm was right in forefront o' biotechnological progress when they was still runnin' about in rompers!"

Old Seth Roentgen, Britain's foremost biotechnologist, has every right to be scornful. At an Open Day at the Ohm Farm this week he sat chuckling proudly in his nuclear-powered rocking chair as Bert Fischbein, his head stockman, led out the new, state-of-the-art Bovomat Mark IV, the latest model of the all-purpose beef cow that was banned from Smithfield Show on safety grounds as long ago as 1974.

This new, genetically modified Bovomat, which weighs about 180 stone and is handled by remote control, can provide ready-sliced Olde Englisshe Taverne-style roast beef to any degree of thickness or rareness required, together with horse-radish sauce, synthetic gravy, Yorkshire pudding, roast potatoes and choice of three vegetables, all served on traditional jumbo-size platters, at the touch of a button.

It can also offer "Soup of the Day", roll and butter (made up in neat, hygienic packets); choice of treacle sponge pudding or Black Forest cherry gateau; genetically modified pint of beer or "wine-type" wine by the glass; and coffee in the lounge. Recorded badinage by Mine Host is optional.

At yesterday's demonstration, Fischbein inadvertently pressed the wrong combination of buttons and the Bovomat exploded, showering everybody with genetically modified material which, Old Seth explained, had been proved beneficial to health by 1,500 top-ranking American and British scientists.

"'Tes early days yet," he said, laying a gnarled forefinger to an even more gnarled nose. "Bound to be teethin' troubles, headaches to iron out, look you, ba gum, och awa', begorrah, me liddle ol' darlin' isn't it?"

He is one of the few remaining speakers of the old composite British dialect, and is under contract with the English Tourist Board to speak it whenever required.

Respect

Why are the most violent and horrible football hooligans officially classed as "Category C"? Keith Nobes, newly appointed visiting professor of football hooligan studies at Soup Hales University, explains: "This system of classification, which is believed to have been codified at a joint seminar at Woodhall Spa by police experts and specialists in the football fan behavioural studies faculty of the Football Association, baffles many hooligans themselves.

"Some, who are not too sure of the order of the letters in the alphabet, keep what we may call an open mind. But others, though proud to belong to 'Category C', think that, as they are superior to other hooligans, they should be called 'Category A' and so entitled to more, like, respect.

"Disputes between hooligans as to which category they belong to, or ought to belong to, can lead to nasty incidents. I myself am classified 'Category B', my main 'medium', as we call it, being ripping out seats in the stadiums without actually hurling them about, and moderate, like, obscene language.

"As such, though I get patronised by 'Category C', I get respect from 'Category A' hooligans, who only hurl things like cigarette packets, use expletives like 'bloody hell' and get practically no respect at all.

"However, the one thing all hooligans agree on is keeping to your own rank. Only yesterday, down at the boozer, I made some rather amusing remarks, as I thought, about a big hooligan I took to be of no category at all.

"When he turned out to belong to a special 'Category Z' he had invented for himself, I had to run for it. Talk about respect!"

Dig

Did man originate in Africa or appear in different varieties in different parts of the world? This question, with its terrible "racist" implications, was discussed by 700 palaeontologists from 75 countries at a conference in South Africa last weekend.

Dr John Goodbone, head of the palaeontology department at Nerdley University, took no part in the conference. But he has not been idle.

In a hastily organised weekend "dig" at his favourite site near the Star of Bangladesh Takeaway Curry Institute on the old Nerdley bypass, he quickly unearthed remains that he claims are "at least five years older" than the earliest hominid remains so far known, which are said to date back 4.4 million years.

Dr Goodbone, who over the past few years has discovered, on the same site, *Homo Nerdliensis*, *Homo Souphaliensis*, *Homo Eosouphaliensis* and many other hominids dating further and further back, has named his new find *Homo Protosouphaliensis*.

But, he says, there is nothing to worry about. Examination of the remains shows that the hominid was "completely multi-racial and multi-cultural". This new "missing link", he believes, had several unusual characteristics.

Examination of the skull shows that it had no space for a brain at all. This would have prevented it from thinking unwelcome or inconvenient thoughts. On the other hand, it had an exceptionally large mouth, probably capable of delivering statements without time-wasting cerebration.

Several of the teeth appear to have been stopped with dental amalgam. This, Dr Goodbone thinks, may mean "we shall have to revise our views on the state of metallurgy and dentistry more than four million years ago". A glass eye was also found, "posing questions central to our understanding of the status of opticians in early society".

Did these peculiarities account for this hominid's survival in the face of extreme weather conditions, continual volcanic eruptions, tidal waves and marauding dinosaurs?

As Dr Goodbone says: "A palaeontologist visiting the site of what is now Nerdley by-pass four million years ago might be struck by the absence of many things we now take for granted, such as petrol stations, snack bars, football fans and, of course, palaeontologists."

Dope

The use of heroin among the young is said to be spreading from run-down estates and "inner cities" to provincial towns and even country areas. So there is great talk of the Government's "focusing its anti-drugs strategy" on this new threat. True to form, Keith Hellawell, the "anti-drugs co-ordinator", declares with supreme banality that "the first thing is to recognise that there is a problem".

The next thing is to recognise that there isn't a solution. No amount of strategy and focusing and co-ordination will stop people taking drugs. There is no tribe on Earth, however primitive, which has not discovered, often with remarkable ingenuity, some kind of drug to ease the pain of existence or induce agreeable or illusory states of mind.

It is likely that, when Adam and Eve were expelled from Paradise, the first thing they did was to search for some substance that would make them imagine that they were back there.

What the official drugs strategists often ignore about drugs is the most obvious thing about them: that they give their users immense pleasure.

In our tolerant society every agency of persuasion is devoted, often exclusively, to making young people believe that the main purpose of living is to secure the greatest possible amount of pleasure, most readily through drugs and sex.

How can any official propaganda campaign prevail against the inclinations of those who have learnt that lesson only too well? How can any moral authority — and moral authority itself is dwindling under concerted attack — persuade them to change their ways or take heed of dire, but often misleading, warnings of what will happen to them if they don't?

The Western world has given itself up wholeheartedly to the great principle of hedonism. How can that be changed — except, of course, by some catastrophe, which would change everything and "solve the drugs problem" in a grim and possibly final way?

Project

One of the objects of the United Nations presence in Bosnia is supposed to be to restore the multiracial — or more correctly multicultural — society that existed there before the civil war.

In so far as this really did exist in the old Yugoslavia, I suppose it will have been a matter of the people belonging to the different communities — Serb, Croat and Muslim — getting on together reasonably well most of the time, as people often do if they are left to attend to their own affairs.

But the war has produced such hatred among these people that any return to that imperfect but tolerable past must be impossible. Most of them, apart from politicians, careerist officials and the lone *Independent* reader in Sarajevo, will not want to be citizens of the fictitious, multicultural state of "Bosnia" which the thinkers of the United Nations have invented for them.

Yet in order to impose this fiction on the natives, the United Nations — that is, the United States — maintains a powerful military force there, including many British troops.

It uses every method of persuasion, from lecturing them on "human rights" and the appropriate way of behaving in the modern world to bombing them from the air, shooting those who are designated "war criminals" or kidnapping them for trial by a court arbitrarily set up at the Hague on behalf of a fictitious "world community".

When this kind of thing occurs among individuals, it is often called "projection". Because we in the West, particularly in America, are supposed to live in multicultural societies, but do not really like the idea all that much, we must at any cost create for the people of Bosnia a model state, an entity that somebody (a wicked Serb, no doubt) has called "a multicultural theme park".

Though nominally for the benefit of the Bosnians, it is really for the comfort of ourselves. And if they don't like it, they can lump it.

Bookshelf

As the anniversary of the death of Diana, Princess of Wales approaches, publishers are becoming desperate. Viper and Bugloss alone has published more than 50 new books about her in the past month, ranging from massive photographic collections to specialised studies on aspects of Diana's life, from nail varnish to post-modern philosophy.

Here are a few of their latest offerings: *The Scientist Princess*, by Karen Oldblatt, reader in women's studies at Nerdley University, deals with the Princess's keen interest in science and her anxiety that the work of women scientists, so unfairly neglected in the past, should be recognised as at least equal to that of men. According to Oldblatt, most of the discoveries attributed to such scientists as Faraday and Einstein were really made by the women assistants they despised, exploited and often beat within an inch of their lives.

A very different book is *Diana as I Knew Her: an Octogenarian Remembers*, by Don Handcough. How believable is the author's account of his frequent encounters with the Princess in the course of his life, on rain-soaked rambles in the Lake District, at darts sessions in West Riding pubs or on Darby and Joan club coach outings to Redcar and Bridlington? Some readers may be sceptical, but most will enjoy these racy memories of a long and senseless life.

More controversial is Leroy Nobes's *Was Diana Black?*. The author is a senior ethnic minorities liaison outreach executive in the race relations department of Soup Hales Borough Council. With painstaking research on scraps of paper and old jam jar labels he discovered in the basement of a derelict Kettering boot factory, he builds up a fascinating theory about a freed black slave girl who, he believes, may have worked in the kitchens of nearby Althorp in the early 18th century, and therefore, he maintains, must have borne a child by the then head of the Spencer family

Not all historians will be convinced. But whether Nobes is right or wrong, this hitherto unsuspected strain in the Princess's ancestry, however remote, can only enhance her status as a compassionate and caring icon for multi-racial Britain.

Pluralism

"A pluralist parliament for a pluralist people" is David Trimble's hope for Northern Ireland, with these mild, well meaning — if somewhat modish — terms replacing the stern old injunction "a Protestant parliament for a Protestant people". And who, you may ask, will be black-hearted enough to quarrel with that?

Pluralism is all the rage at the moment. But when the pluralism that has cast a blight on such tunes as *Rule Britannia* takes hold in Ulster, what will become of the glorious old sectarian songs? Will it be *The Pluralist Boys* and *The Old Pluralist Flute*? When the sash their fathers wore is pluralist, will it still be brave and beautiful?

Will the Irish of the republic have to go pluralist, too, change the tenor of their songs, forget their tragic, romantic history and merge their traditions in the pluralist, global future that we are all instructed to acclaim?

Will even they in the end, in Yeats's phrase, turn "all that great past to a trouble of fools"?

Only connect

A report from the Speech, Language and Hearing Centre recommends that parents speak to their babies for at least half an hour a day, even when they are too young to reply, because it will make them into more intelligent adults. That is all very well, but what should the parents talk about? Experts differ.

Dr Heinz Kiosk, the eminent social psychologist, says parents should talk to their babies, but for much more than half an hour a day, on the evils of racism, sexism and homophobia. "I would suggest six hours a day and whenever babies wake up at night. If they cannot reply, so much the better. They cannot begin too early to absorb unquestioningly, even though subconsciously, the essentials of good citizenship. White, male, middle-class babies particularly need to take on their proper inheritance of guilt."

Dr Llewelyn Goth-Jones, director of community medicine for Stretchford and star of the popular GPI sex programme Calling Doctor Llew, recommends daily talk on sex education and the necessity of safe sex, plus demonstrations on the use of the condom, to make babies aware of the social and economic importance of contraception. His own booklet, *Talk Sex to Your Baby*, may be had from any of his sex advice and abortion clinics (£1.50, post free).

Paul Ohm, the freelance technologist and designer of the All-technological Garden at Edgbaston: "Make your baby more aware of the supreme importance of science by talking at every opportunity about such topics as molecular physics and evolutionary psychology."

Kevin Himmler, formerly coach to Stretchford United FC: "Talk to your baby about football all the time — the tragedy of Hoddle, beset by envious pygmies and baffled by spirit messages; the woes of Gazza as he stumbles disconsolately through the wilderness of the world; and many another stirring, character-forming epic tale."

Ever Onward

In future, English cathedrals may be allowed to protect their "images" by registered trademark. One of the first bishops to act on this is Dr Spaceley-Trellis, the go-ahead Bishop of Stretchford and Bevindon.

The original Gothic cathedral of his diocese, mainly built in the 14th century, collapsed through some timely subsidence soon after he took over.

Had he realised then what a valuable tourist asset the old cathedral would have been, he might have made more effort to preserve it.

However, he believes it is useless to repine, or to regret that no Rogers or Libeskind was around in those days to design a glorious new "post-modern" cathedral, expressing in its jagged disharmony and collapsing planes "the essential values of a secular religion to meet the needs of the average man and woman of today".

He had to be content with the then famous architect Sir Edwin Spasholm (of the Spasholm, Oldbun, Gibberdish Partnership), who designed the present cathedral to the bishop's own specifications.

In its day, it was a truly revolutionary house of worship, a towering yet blockish concrete structure, in which traditional features — nave, aisles, choir, chapels, altars — were all adapted to modern educational and social requirements.

Dr Trellis's steadfast "multifaith" ideals (he is now chairman of Football Managers for a Multifaith Millennium) are reflected throughout the interior, which can be used equally for Christian, Muslim, Buddhist, animist, agnostic, atheist or any other contemporary religious or non-religious purposes.

The People's Narthex incorporates a contraceptive and abortion clinic and sex education cinema. The High Altar can accommodate scientific experiments or publicity displays for the United Nations. The theme of the great West Window, designed by Eileen Ogbufe, is the "Triumph of Humanist Faith".

The cathedral trademark, whether on tea-towels, mugs, tins of fudge or condoms, will be easily distinguishable from those of such cathedrals as York, Ely or Wells, which, as Dr Trellis says, "offer an unhelpful atmosphere of fusty medieval superstition. The image of Stretchford Cathedral will appeal to forward-looking people throughout the world as unmistakably relevant and meaningful in a very real sense."

Impasse

In the spacious morning-room at Marxmount, her fine white mansion on the edge of the Heath, among the trophies of a lifetime of service to peace and higher living standards for the People, Mrs Dutt-Pauker, the eminent Hampstead thinker, sat musing with quiet joy on the predicament of her old enemy, Augusto Pinochet.

Through the tall windows, in the pale December sunlight, she could see Mackenzie the gardener moving among the well-kept parterres and cedared lawns of her domain.

This reminded her of the day after Pinochet's coup, when she ordered Mackenzie to remove all plants of Chilean origin from the garden. Those were the days when she campaigned to ban Chilean wine and other evil products.

It was not quite the same, of course, as banning the evil products of South Africa. For one thing, she found she could not use the faculty (absurdly described by friends as "paranormal", when, of course, there must have been a perfectly valid scientific explanation) of detecting South African goods by their sinister effluvia at distances up to five miles.

She remembered how Allende the martyr had been so cruelly overthrown. Dear Salvador! He had often been her guest at Marxmount, as well as at Glynstalin, her Welsh home, at Craig Gramscie in Scotland and Leninmore in County Kerry.

How often they had talked into the small hours of his plans for a Chilean revolution! And how the children, particularly Deirdre, had loved the gallant young Chilean's colourful talk of how he would forcibly expropriate the rich from their estates when he came to power!

After Allende's fall, she had done her best to save the oppressed workers and peasants of Chile from starvation, by helping fugitives from the Pinochet Terror — some of them were American communists and old friends — to settle in England and carry on the struggle.

And now she found herself positively laughing out loud as she thought of the misadventures of the monster, driven from the London Clinic to asylum in boring north London, and now to the fearfully vulgar, nouveau riche Wentworth Estate in Surrey.

Would he be forced, she wondered, to share the company of the likes of the Duchess of York, Bruce Forsyth, Michael Parkinson and Russ Abbot, a stand-up comedian (whatever that might be)? According to Deirdre, all these frightfully common people were, or at one time had been, residents of that ghastly neighbourhood.

It was in this state of benign amusement that Deirdre found her that morning. And it was her mother's jokes about Pinochet's predicament that put an idea into her head. There must surely be some enjoyable demonstrations going on against the fascist general in his Surrey hideout? Why not join them?

Soon she was in the Marxmount banner store, rummaging among the old insignia — "Hands off Nicaragua!", "Bomb Rhodesia!", "Release Mandela!" and even older ones, her mother's historical favourites, a mouldering "Arms for Spain!" or "Open Second Front Now!" — until she found the one she was looking for: "Ban Chilean Nitrates!" But was it still relevant? Mummy would know.

Blundering into the morning-room with the unwieldy thing and knocking to the floor a valuable bibelot, a silver-mounted strand of souvenir barbed wire from a Soviet labour camp for enemies of the people, she found her mother's mood abruptly changed.

"What on earth will that do to bring Pinochet to justice and restore socialism to Chile?" she hissed. Anger mantled her withered Hegelian cheeks and the lines of dialectic deepened around her materialistic nose. "How often must I tell you, Deirdre, not to meddle with things you know absolutely nothing whatever about?"

Your TV Tonight

GPI network: 6.30pm: The Tubers — will lesbian "right-to-roam" activist Jill join forces with gay paralibrarian Mitch to defy footpath-block-ing homophobe Lord Haversnake? 7pm: The Gay Pharaohs — eminent archaeologists discuss new discoveries showing that the pyramids and other monuments of Ancient Egypt may have been built as committed statements for equal homosexual rights.

8.30pm: Outed — weekly programme in which leading historians reveal the true sexual orientation of famous men and women of history. This week: Charlemagne, Nell Gwynne, Winston Churchill. 9.30pm: European tax harmonisation and the gay community. 10.30pm: Soup Hales Gay and Lesbian Youth Orchestra plays music by gay and lesbian composers. 11.30pm: Hear All Sides — homophobia in the media and the scandal of censorship.

On a Visit

In China, Clare Short, described as an International Development Secretary, declined to lobby on behalf of British firms. "There was some suggestion that I might raise the odd contract that came around. I didn't bother."

In a thoughtful article by "A Noblewoman", *The Feudal Times and Reactionary Herald* comments: "All who cherish good manners and good feeling, and deplore the present decline in both, will commend Miss Short's attitude.

"Of humble origin herself, she evidently aspires, and most laudably, to the higher standards of a past age, when to be 'in trade' carried a certain social stigma, and rightly so.

"Again we must commend Miss Short for her statement, however oddly expressed, that her 'job' is to defend 'the human rights of the poorest people in the world'.

"We are sure she means to model herself on all those ladies of gentle birth who in the past devoted themselves, often risking great danger and discomfort, to alleviating the lot of the poor and unfortunate in distant lands.

"May we point out, however, that charity begins at home? In the intervals of her expeditions to uncivilised parts of the world, might she not attend, in the spirit of that unjustly derided character, Lady Bountiful, to the poor and unfortunate at home, whether in rural cottage or factory worker's dwelling?

"A personal visit to such people, bearing warm clothing, hot soup, puddings and other nourishing comestibles, would encourage them to accept their humble lot with courage and endurance, and show them that those of higher station are not too proud to visit them in a sympathetic and gracious spirit.

"What a beautiful and uplifting picture! On a dull, freezing winter's day, when the spirits of even the well born may sink a little, Miss Short alights from her carriage with her charitable offerings!

"How the little ragged children run out to greet her with glad cries! How even the bedridden old crone within raises a feeble yet heartfelt groan of welcome! Yes, it is at such moments as these that we can truly say: noblesse oblige!"

Industrial News

A report by a former commissioner of the Commission for Racial Equality accuses it of spending "vast sums of public money achieving very little other than self-promotion and self-perpetuation".

This ought not to worry workers in the mighty race relations industry. It is the proof, if proof were needed, that it is indeed an industry and, like many industries, is primarily concerned not so much with providing useful goods or services as with its own growth.

It is this dynamic spirit of enterprise that, in 40 years, has raised it from small beginnings to become "Britain's Economic Growthpoint No 1".

And it is still growing. The other day, in a sensational breakthrough, the Court of Appeal found that a white woman who left her job with a van hire company, because she objected to its discrimination against black and Asian clients, was thereby herself a victim of racial discrimination. An industrial tribunal awarded her £5,000 for constructive dismissal. Is this the first known case of "vicarious" or "secondary" racism?

It opens up a vast new field for the race relations industry to exploit, imposing a yet heavier burden of neurotic guilt and fear on English people. It will bring new joy to the higher race relations theorists working away in the cloud-capped towers of Ethnic House, the industry's London headquarters.

Will "vicarious racism" prove to be the "missing force" in their long-sought grand unified field theory of race relations? Is "racism" inherent in the very structure of the universe?

Whack

Caught in a riot by Muslim demonstrators in Cape Town last week, the Prime Minister remarked easily: "You get used to them. It was pretty limited and there were a very small number of demonstrators."

Meanwhile, relatives of Muslim British subjects, mostly from Birmingham and arrested as terrorist suspects in Yemen, have threatened that, if the men are not fairly treated, there will be "blood on the streets". And Sheikh Abu Hamza, leader of a London-based Muslim radical group, says in a playfully sinister way that, if the British obstruct the group's activities, they can expect a "whack".

From small beginnings great things grow. Ten years ago, when the Ayatollah Khomeini pronounced his fatwa against Salman Rushdie, radical Muslims in England called for Rushdie's death — a clear case of incitement to murder, which is a serious crime under English law. But nobody was prosecuted.

It is no doubt true, as we are often told, that the great majority of Muslims in England are peaceable, law-abiding people who want only to mind their own business and have nothing to do with potentially violent radical Muslim causes.

But the progress of any successful terrorist movement, as in Ireland, has a hideous logic. It works by the contagion of hatred and excitement and, as it grows stronger, by the systematic intimidation of ordinary, helpless people. A time may come — God forbid that it ever should — when Blair may have to get even more used to Muslim riots and demonstrations; when politicians' accustomed boasts of the glories of our "multiracial, multicultural society" may sound even more fatuous than they do now.

Nature Diary

By '*Redshank*'

"Watercolourists do be out by Hundred Acre Bottom," said Old Jim, the retired poacher ominously, when I met him yesterday morning in my customary walk in search of prematurely nesting birds who might need a helping hand. Used as we are to seeing these strange people in our parts, I had never before glimpsed them in the very depth of winter, when all colour seems drained from the landscape.

What can they find to paint at such a season? Yet there they were, a band of some 50 men and women with their easels and paintboxes, muffled against the cold and tottering over the fields to take up position nigh to Blumber's Oak. These people, many of them elderly, to judge from their faint, peevish cries of discomfort, come trooping from the nearby town as though by some weird compulsion.

Some are what the country folk call "people with learning difficulties released into the community".

I watched as they set out their apparatus and began painting, some lackadaisically, others in frantic haste, as a big, ginger-haired fellow in his seventies, who seemed to have authority over them, kept bawling out orders: "Watch your diagonals there! More Chinese white! Cut out that rose madder! Try to feel the chiaroscuro!"

As he strode about in his heavy watercolourist's boots, occasionally dabbing confidently with an outsize brush at his own version of the landscape, he seemed to demand not merely obedience but fear.

Some of the group were close to tears. But I knew better than to interfere, even though, as I strolled on over the hills, I could hear the big watercolourist's voice rising to sergeant-major pitch.

Country folk believe that these watercolourists are creatures of ill omen who must at all costs be kept away from human habitations. I sometimes think that such rural beliefs encapsulate a profound, age-old wisdom for ever beyond the grasp of your average cocksure urban intellectual.

Other Worlds

Not content with threatening the outermost planet, Pluto, with loss of its planetary status, astronomers are suggesting that its only moon, Charon, may have once supported life or may now be habitable. Daguerreotypes transmitted from the columnar space-vehicle, Don Carlos and the Holy Alliance III, now motoring through the Solar System, indicate that Charon, described by these scientists as just an icy sphere 790 miles across, is not merely inhabitable, but is a delightful little inhabited world of its own.

It seems that the hereditary landowners who hold the great estates on Pluto, where a race of burly, ruddy-cheeked peasants till the land in immemorial contentment, have taken over Charon and made it into a small sportsman's paradise. Beautifully diversified with hill and dale, it has grouse moors, deer forests, pheasant coverts and acres of grassland where small game abound.

There are sparkling streams well stocked with fish and, here and there, standing on rocky outcrops or embowered in noble trees, there are what seem to be agreeable chalets and hunting lodges, with comfortable quarters well furnished with trophies, whisky decanters and leather-bound volumes of the *Plutonian Gentleman's Magazine*. The daguerreotypes await further interpretation. But there is enough evidence to suggest that, as we have long suspected, astronomy, like other sciences, is purely subjective.

Balance

Anxious to keep viewers informed on subjects they might not otherwise have heard about, the GPI Television Network is presenting a series of carefully balanced programmes on the theme "Racism and the Police". In fact, apart from its usual three-second news bulletins, chat shows and homosexual education programmes, it is broadcasting nothing else this week.

A real treat for viewers this evening (8-10pm) is a revival of Neville Dreadberg's brilliant award-winning documentary masterpiece *Monsters in Blue*, first broadcast in the 1970s, when it caused a sensation with its revelations of police corruption, drugs and arms smuggling, extortion, systematic use of torture, cannibalism and mass murder.

Brilliant playwright, novelist, designer, photographer, chef, film director, composer, hairdresser and multimedia self-publicist Dreadberg has produced, at short notice, a new, up-to-date version of his historic documentary.

In this new version, almost all the victims of police terror are blacks or Asians. The climax, which carries a stunning dramatic impact, shows how a gang of typical policemen snatch a passing black man off the street, drag him to the police station, dismember him, cook him in the canteen kitchen and eat him, with evident relish, amid uproarious "canteen culture" jokes.

From 10pm onwards, GPI is putting out another of its popular Hear All Sides discussion programmes. The subject is "The Policeman: the Enemy in our Midst?" Taking part are Dr Wendy Dutt-Pauker, Head of Anti-Police Studies at Stretchford University; Tamsin Alibi-Jones of the Race Relations Industrial Council; Greg Blowhard, head of the Anti-racism Demonstrational Department at Gnomesall Heath University; Royston Huitzilopochtli, South Shields-born sociologist and leader of the Nerdley Aztec community; Dr E J T Spacely-Trellis, Bishop of Stretchford; and Dr Abdul Castrumba, Emeritus Professor of Social Subversion at Soup Hales University.

At a hastily summoned press conference, Sir Godfrey Fobster, chairman of GPI, said: "We are already getting the usual dreary bleats about 'bias' from stick-in-the-mud Tory backwoodsmen, monocled foxhunting thugs, ghastly reactionary middle-class male white morons and their even more ghastly wives, and neo-Nazis from the so-called countryside.

"I sometimes wonder whether there's any point in trying to humour these horrible, brain-dead bigots. But we at GPI have a remit, which we cherish dearly, to be impartial at all costs.

"So after midnight we shall broadcast a three-minute interview by arts co-ordinator and Labour councillor Pippa Dreadberg, Neville's brilliant wife, with a 76-year-old retired police constable, Jack Smith, who is undergoing a course of electro-convulsive therapy for acute depression."

Sporting Life

"Tony" Banks, who holds the preposterous title "minister of sport", announces that chess is to be officially recognised as a sport. Will this mean a revival of chess as it was played 20 years ago in the Stretchford Conurbation? In those days, they played the league game, described as "distinguishable from Rugby League football only by its infinitely greater violence".

People still remember the legendary cup final of 1980 between Nerdley Chess Circle and Soup Hales Boardsmen at the old Bradlaugh Memorial Stadium. As the Stretchford Clarion vividly reported, "the match started with an ominous lull, a sure sign to the cognoscenti of trouble ahead.

"Sure enough, in the 11th minute all hell broke loose at the famed number three board as Soup Hales striker Ron Osmosis (White) was warned by referee Stan Ulbricht for kicking Nerdley's Jim Vissarionovitch on the kneecap while castling illegally after moving his king. At once a furious Osmosis claimed that his king had been moved not by him but by a magnetic force emanating from the Nerdley stands.

"Within seconds, fans of both sides invaded the playing area, shouldering players and even chessmen aside and turning the stadium into a horrific melange of flying fists, lead-weighted pieces and exploding clocks before setting it on fire.

"Then followed the traditional 'end game' rampage through the neighbourhood, with its grim legacy of trampled gardens, broken windows, toppled chimneys and piles of rubble that will take the nearby residents days to clear up — some of it radioactive, and needing to be tested with makeshift home-made Geiger counters."

"These people are like animals," commented more than 27,000 residents, while an estimated 8,000 stated: "They are worse than animals. Animals don't play chess."

Perhaps owing to adverse public reactions, chess on this scale gradually lost out to the rival attractions of dwarf-throwing, professional vandalism and synchronised boring. Once-famous stars like Vissarionovitch faded away. At a recent reunion of players and hooligans, he appeared a wizened, creaking, arthritic old man. Challenged to play against his old rival Osmosis, he tried to move his queen's pawn, then, overcome by fatigue, fell forward over the board and had to be revived by a crack team of chess paramedics.

Now that chess is to be recognised as a proper sport, with all that implies, will those old days return, with a new, far more up-to-date cast of millionaire grandmasters, even more violent hooligans, corrupt officials, call girls and all the other glories of sport today? Already there are reports of "sexual harassment" of women players. Now that is a thing which would have shocked even the most brutish old-time hooligan to the core.

Appeal

"Smokers Kill 125 Babies a Year" says a heading. Figures given out in a campaign (called "Smoking: Give up for Kids"), to make parents aware of the dangers of "passive smoking" as a cause of cot deaths, indicate that a baby is eight times more likely to succumb to cot death if both parents smoke.

Dr Ron Hardware and his dedicated team of research scientists at Nerdley University believe that all cot deaths, and most other childhood ills, are caused by passive smoking, though not necessarily by parents.

Babies are also at risk from smoking visitors and relations (the figure for uncle-related cot deaths alone may be as high as six a year), or from people smoking in passing cars at distances of up to 30 miles.

"Our main headache," Dr Hardware says, "is that we are not yet allowed to experiment on the babies themselves, even though many parents are anxious to offer us their babies for the sake of scientific progress and a healthy, non-smoking future for all.

"In the meantime," he says with growing emphasis, even with something threatening in his tone, "we urgently need extra resources — extra laboratory equipment, extra personnel — if we are to crack this huge problem of passive smoking and cot death once and for all.

"Above all, we need more money. It is scandalous that vital scientific research should be starved of funds in this way. A crash programme of research, with a generous government grant, would make a start . . ."

Stealth

Whether merely misguided or positively wicked, but in either case doing nothing much to help the wretched, doubly victimised Albanians, the war in Serbia is decidedly short on laughs, even on gallows humour. But I liked a newspaper photograph, which showed two Serbian women dancing a jig on the wreckage of an American "Stealth" fighter that had crashed near their village.

Milling around in the background were a lot of smiling villagers, eager to hack off a few souvenirs from the wreckage for their children and grandchildren to marvel at. These people were described in the report as "peasants". But they looked very much like the sort of people you would come across at any small country show in England.

They could hardly have realised what a wonderful piece of symbolism they were enacting. Here were simple people under attack from a bogus "International Community", part of some unfathomable world strategy.

Did they guess, as they danced on the wreckage of that evil-looking machine — that triumph of American military technology — that its value in dollars was greater by far than the value of their whole village and their whole neighbourhood, themselves included?

Without knowing it, they had won a small, symbolic victory for the humble people of the world against overbearing power. They were right to rejoice, however briefly.

We should rejoice with them. Apart from our common humanity, mightn't we wake up one day to find that we were under attack from some bogus "International Community" ourselves?

Mother's Help

Thoughtful young mothers are wondering about potential au pair girls among any Albanian refugees arriving in this country. Probably the best known Albanian au pair already working here is Gjoq, who looks after Deirdre Dutt-Pauker's bearded little activist son, Bert Brecht Ho Che Banana, at Marxmount, the family mansion on the edge of Hampstead Heath.

Gjoq, who is a Stalinist from northern Albania, is 6ft 4in, a stately daughter of Eve with what terrified suitors have called "an irresistible, Medusa-like beauty". Two years ago, on holiday in her native land, she applied to join the then nascent Kosovo Liberation Army.

But in spite of first-rate qualifications for guerrilla warfare, gained in the unending conflict with the Maoist Bert behind the green-baize door of the nursery wing — home-made flame-throwers and rocket-launchers have been used on both sides — she was turned down.

When she suggested that the KLA should kill such "moderates" as Ibrahim Rugova straight away, instead of saving them up so that the Serbs could be accused of killing them later on, even the hardest of the hard men were shocked.

Quailing when she dismissed them as "a pathetic bunch of fluffies", they were relieved to see the back of her. But if the Americans fall for her unusual charms, she may still rise to supreme power in a future Greater Albania.

Empire

"We are all internationalists now," says Tony Blair, "whether we like it or not."

"The great battle of our time," says his Master, Bill Clinton, "pits the forces of globalism against those of tribalism." This, in their own words, is the doctrine that drives these eminent windbags on in their barbarous war against the Serbian people.

It is also the doctrine that all people of goodwill are supposed to believe in. What could be clearer? On one side there is globalism: the brotherhood of man, rational, enlightened, pointing the way to a future of universal peace, democracy, justice, benevolence and happiness.

On the other hand there is tribalism: a mass of ancient enmities and hatreds and dark superstitions, source of war without end and of all the miseries and cruelties of the unregenerated human past.

However, it is not as simple as that. What to Blair and Clinton may seem a glimpse of future paradise may seem to others the very worst of nightmares. If such people still cling to their racial, national, tribal and parochial allegiances and attitudes, it is not out of primitive hatred, but because they feel instinctively that their manners and customs, their individuality and identity, even their familiar surroundings, all the things they personally know and understand and love, are threatened by a strange, new, inhuman, global power.

It is the power that ceaselessly disseminates a degenerate mass culture throughout the world, perverting and destroying every local custom and tradition; that exploits every natural resource to meet the demand it perpetually creates for new and superfluous machines and luxuries; tears up with mad, mechanical glee the vestiges of ancient nations; aspires to plan and control the whole world's food supply and rule everything by the power of imaginary money.

We may call that power "America" or "the New World Order" or "the International Community" or what we please. An ancient name for it is the Empire of Mammon.

It may seem irresistible today, but we have it on good authority that in the end it shall not prevail.

Symbols

"What has happened", crows an exultant writer in the *Observer*, "is a decisive and perhaps terminal defeat for an older Europe, a place of tribal hatreds, doubled-headed eagles, flaming swords and obscure martyrs. A better world order survives…"

Everyone to his taste. Along with those ancient, long revered but now execrated symbols of local allegiances, national pride, glory, honour, nobility and beauty, the last of our European civilisation is perishing with all its treasures, giving way to a new world order, a place of internationalism, scientism, heartless accountancy, rationalism, egalitarianism, false humanity-mongering and everything that belongs to the legions of the dull.

But no one should think this new world order will be without powerful symbols of its own. High above the clouds as the state-organised pop festivals and democratic sports rallies proceed amid universal rejoicing, the continual murmur and drone of bombers can be heard. They are double-headed eagles and flaming swords brought up to date for a prosaic people. They are the symbols of the new order, the means by which obedience will be ruthlessly enforced.

ACC XLV

Forty-five years have passed since the foundation of this column. Each year, as the outer world of falsity grows worse, our celebration grows at once more solemn and more jubilant. In the Capital, the deep-toned bells of the Basilica toll as the great abbots and nobles, bearing on their broad shoulders the dreaming loads of Church and State, meet in the Hall of Heroes to receive the tribute of the lesser feudatories.

After them, in order of rank, the lower orders, equally honoured in their fashion in this unchanging hierarchy ("Every man in his place, and a place for every man") offer their more humble tributes. Elders and headmen from the country villages tender symbolic gifts of wine and fruit, sheaves of corn, nuggets of tin and lead, water from sacred wells.

Children from remote mountain villages, reputedly descended from the wild nomad horsemen who once roamed the Northern Wastes on the old frontier, bring garlands, herons' eggs, strangely shaped stones inscribed with indecipherable runes. And all is done as it has been done from the beginning.

In those 45 years, the column has passed through many vicissitudes. No matter. Since it is at once a verbal, metaphorical and territorial entity, what is technically called its "apparent" location cannot affect its "intrinsic" location. Wherever it may "appear" to be — even if it should appear on the women's pages of the *Guardian*, printed upside down, it would still remain intact in its own "space", a realm unchanging and unchangeable.

It is fitting that it should now appear on the very same page of the newspaper on which it first appeared 45 years ago. Then, it was on the eastern frontier of the page; now it is on the western. Now, instead of bordering, as then, the narrow Interpaginal Channel, with a coastline on the Dreaded Northern Void, we have a broad coastline on the equally Dreaded Western and Northern Voids. This is a subject for endless and completely futile speculation for our natural philosophers.

Is there life outside the column?

Ingsoc

"I did what I did with the best intentions", says Mrs Melita Norwood, accused of passing atomic secrets to the Soviet Union. She believed, and went on believing, that the Soviet Union represented the best hope for humanity, because it stood for the principles of socialism and progress.

In that belief she was not alone. In the 1930's, the great majority of what are now called "the chattering classes" were of that belief. So also, in the later parts of the war, when the Soviet Union was officially our ally, were the unthinking public.

It lingered even when the "Cold War" got under way and the horrendous crimes of the Soviet Union became common knowledge. It still persists in a modified form as a belief in the fundamental goodness of socialism. How often have you heard simple-minded people say: "Socialism didn't fail in the Soviet Union — it was never tried".

The Soviet Union might have collapsed. But the belief in socialism and progress that it represented has not collapsed. It does not matter that there is no important political party in England that calls itself "socialist". All the main parties, Labour, Liberal, Conservative, are committed to one basic principle of socialism — equality: sexual, racial, universal — that was official doctrine in the Soviet Union. It is official doctrine in England now.

In the real world, an egalitarian society is unattainable, because real people do not want it. So all attempts to achieve it lead to a system in which everything must be regulated, a bureaucratic totalitarianism, in the case of the Soviet Union shabby, squalid and inefficient. That, with obvious differences, is what we are heading for in England now.

That is why almost everything that happens in the "public domain" in England, from "anti-racist" regulations and compulsory sex education to the destruction of the Monarchy, is an aspect of creeping socialism.

It is proceeding by almost imperceptible steps, first to a "European" and then to a world state, the ultimate triumph of socialism and progress, which, unlike the Soviet Union's projected world empire, might be only too acceptable to an enslaved and conditioned humanity